Heaven on Earth
A Lutheran–Orthodox Odyssey

Robert Tobias

Forewords by
Orthodox Archbishop Iakovos
and
Lutheran Bishop James R. Crumley

Illustrated by John West

Tobias-Wells Endowments

Chickadee

Cover: Andrei Rublev's "The Three Visitors" (Gen. 18), early 15th century, Russian; generally regarded as an icon of the Holy Trinity. Photo by Frank Veber.

First printing, 1996, The American Lutheran Publicity Bureau
ISBN: 0–9633142–9–7
Special Education Edition for Congregations, 1997
Produced by Tobias-Wells Endowments
Distributed by canonical Orthodox dioceses
and Evangelical Lutheran synods
© Copyright 1997 by Robert Tobias
103 South Lakeshore Drive, Racine, WI 53403
All rights reserved.

Cover background images © 1996 PhotoDisc, Inc.
Illustrations and cover photo used by permission of
John West and Frank Veber
Printed in the United States of America

Contents

I crossed a moor, with a name of its own
And a use in the world no doubt,
Yet a hand's breadth of it shines alone
'Mid the blank miles round about:

For there I picked up on the heather
And there I put inside my breast
A moulted feather, an eagle-feather—
Well, I forget the rest.

Robert Browning, "Memorabilia"

Personal Letter to Readers

Grace, peace and joy in God the Father, God the Son, and God the Holy Spirit.

I have prepared this book of anecdotes, plus some spiritual and theological reflections, as a personal supplement to the scholarly reports of our official Lutheran-Orthodox Dialogue in North America. It is intended for use by laity, students, and study groups in local congregations. We hope many will be stimulated to add their reflections and prayers to those of the official Dialogue now at work. Local study groups may find the "Questions for Study Groups" at the end helpful towards that participation.

This Special Education Edition has been produced by Tobias-Wells Endowments with the cooperation of ALPB, publishers of the first printing. It is being distributed courtesy of your own Orthodox diocese or Lutheran synod.

If your pastor or priest already has a copy, congratulations. Sharp pastor! That's enough to start a small (very small) study group. For a growing study group additional copies of the first printing are available from ALPB Books as indicated on the back cover.

We suggest that readers and study groups, unless they are Lutheran historians, skip the Author's "Introduction: a Touch of History," and go straight to Chapter 1, returning to the Introduction as resource material with Chapter 8, "American Culture and Our Commonalities."

We hope you will enjoy the book and will find it rewarding for your own spiritual and theological reflection, as well as helpful in your congregation's educational and ecumenical programs.

Good luck, good digging, and God's blessings. If we can answer any specific questions, feel free to contact us at Tobias-Wells Endowments, 103 South Lakeshore, Racine, WI 53403; (414) 552-8257.

Enjoy Heaven on Earth!

– *Robert Tobias*

Acknowledgments

More than three decades ago His Eminence Archbishop Iakovos, Primate of the Greek Orthodox Church in North and South America, began steps that would lead to a process of official dialogue between Orthodox and Lutheran churches in North America. A decade later he was joined by the Rev. Dr. James R. Crumley, Jr., presiding Bishop of the Lutheran Church in America (now Evangelical Lutheran Church in America). They have been faithful advocates and mentors of that process and its participants ever since. In that same spirit of commitment to their Lord and concern for their churches and for church unity, they have graciously written brief forewords addressed to readers of this book. We are all in their debt.

Father Gregory Wingenbach, Greek Orthodox priest and Executive Director of the Kentuckiana Interfaith Community, after careful reading of the text, kindly provided helpful insights from an Orthodox perspective as well as factual corrections. John West, art director and illustrator, rendered the line drawings that accompany this text. Frank Veber provided the cover photograph. Paul Tobias, graphic artist and founder of Liaison Productions, designed the text layout and contributed his technical expertise to the project. Kathryn Tobias, editor, made helpful comments and suggestions regarding the text. Connie Seddon, editor and board member of the American Lutheran Publicity Bureau, performed the final editing of the book and saw the project through to completion. All these friends collaborated with fine spirit and with consummate skill and patience.

Beyond these named friends and my immediate colleagues, to whom I am most grateful, a host of Orthodox faithful in this country and abroad, from children and refugees to kings and patriarchs, have been most gracious and hospitable and have patiently introduced me to Orthodoxy over the past fifty years. The doors and windows that they have opened have been a rich blessing to our entire family, to my students, associates, friends, and, I trust, to readers of this book. To them all and, finally, to the American Lutheran Publicity Bureau whose vision and commitment made the first publication of this book a reality, I offer a most hearty *Eucharisto polu!*

Forewords

H *eaven on Earth: A Lutheran–Orthodox Odyssey* by a scholarly friend, the Rev. Robert Tobias, is a real challenge addressed to both Lutherans and Orthodox Christians to embark upon a spiritual odyssey with the compass fixed at discovering one another and a common refreshed concern: the reuniting of the church of Christ. The Rev. Tobias has always tried to contribute toward that end as much as any ecumenically minded clergyman would do.

My acquaintance and friendship with Bob goes back to 1955 to 17 Route de Malagnou in Geneva where the Lutheran World Federation was one of the branches of the World Council of Churches. It was there where both of us met and expressed the wish that the Orthodox–Lutheran Dialogue, which was instituted in the 16th century, should be resumed and continued. Being then young dreamers and wanderers, we decisively set our goal to rediscover Ithaca, where a Penelope—the long-awaiting ecumenical thought and nostalgia—would find its fulfillment.

At last, in 1965, thanks to Rev. Tobias, our first meeting was made possible in New York, which drew the map and planned the course for the resumption of the interrupted 16th-century conversation between the Orthodox and the Lutherans.

The overseer of our ship is the same lovingly caring Jesus Christ. If I read correctly His lips, He is addressing us with the reprimanding question: "Men of little faith, why do you hesitate?" The book of Rev. Robert Tobias challenges us with the same agonizing question. Don't you think it is time to boldly approach our unfinished dialogue?

ARCHBISHOP IAKOVOS

Primate of the Greek Orthodox Church
of North and South America

When I was elected bishop of the Lutheran Church in America, my contacts with the Orthodox church had been minimal and what I knew of its history was quite superficial. Yet, of all of my experiences as bishop, I list those with the Orthodox church and its members among the most important, both for me personally and for the church that I represented. Member churches formerly of the Lutheran Council in the U.S.A. and currently members of the Lutheran World Federation have been engaged in serious theological dialogue with many other churches for more than three decades. What we have learned has been most heartening for those who are convinced that the visible expression of the unity of the church must have a high priority. We have developed consensus on crucial matters we had assumed to be church-dividing.

Especially with the Orthodox churches, unity in the faith is manifested in many ways. We "do theology" differently. Yet, we find that in the concern and life of the church and of the believers we hold much in common. And even when I have found it difficult to understand and to experience what was related to me by the Orthodox, I have been quick to admire and to respect.

This "anecdotal account" by Robert Tobias is profoundly illustrative of the journey we must make. It involves the people who confess the faith. I will always be deeply indebted to Archbishop Iakovos for the way he received me as a Christian brother and bishop. In our many associations, he referred to himself as "James the Elder" (*Iakovos* in Greek) and to me as "James the Younger." It was his way of proclaiming our mutual discipleship. Through his urging, I visited all of the Orthodox patriarchates, talked with the patriarchs and their staffs, worshiped in their liturgies, enjoyed their hospitality. My life was changed in those encounters and my faith greatly enlarged.

It is by God's gracious invitation that we participate in His life, "in Christ." By the same grace, we participate in the lives of one another, "in Christ." Robert Tobias testifies to the way that has happened in his life and experience. I can only hope and pray that it would be true for all of us.

BISHOP JAMES R. CRUMLEY, JR.

Evangelical Lutheran Church in America

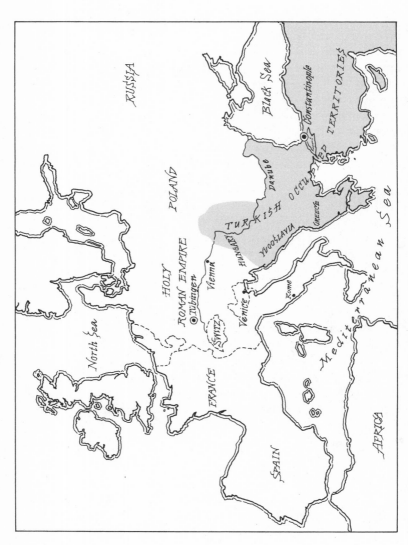

Central Europe at the time of the Jeremias–Tübingen correspondence, 1576–1581

Introduction: A Touch of History

This anecdotal account of some of my experiences with Orthodox fellow Christians, mostly in East Europe but also in North America, is intended for students, laity, and clergy, especially in the Orthodox and Lutheran traditions. It is a supplement to the scholarly publications of our official dialogues. A few preliminary bits of history[1] may help illuminate the personal events and reflections reported here.

In the spring of 1946, between World War II and the Cold War, I found myself conferring with fellow Christians in East Europe. Mine was a double mission: one, for the World Council of Churches (in Process of Formation), to observe the needs and prospects of East European churches as Soviet forces began their postwar occupation of the area; the second, for the newly formed World Federation of Democratic Youth, to establish bonds of understanding between young people worldwide in the aftermath of World War II. Communication that had been disrupted in World War II by Nazi censorship was once again intense, gracious, heart-warming. Very shortly thereafter, formal contact between Christians of the West and Orthodox Christians in East Europe was again cut off, this time by Soviet occupation. But communication was not. "Therefore with angels and

[1]A detailed expansion of these notes from history will be found in J. Meyendorff and R. Tobias, eds., *Salvation in Christ: A Lutheran-Orthodox Dialogue, Vol. II* (Evangelical Lutheran Church in America, Chicago, IL, 1994).

archangels and with all the company of heaven ...," continuity and communication were still there and profoundly experienced, transcending political and military censorships.

Relationships During the Reformation

In the 1500s, when the bonds between the Lutheran reformers and the Vatican were broken, the reformers were formally cut off from historic continuity in the church. They felt that deeply, and soon looked to the Orthodox East for the possibility of restored historic continuity. Martin Luther himself had no direct contact with Eastern Orthodoxy, but he held the Eastern church in very high regard. He was familiar with the writings of the early Fathers, quoted them in his writings and lectures, and held—against Catholic theologian John Eck— that the "Greek Church" had produced more and better theologians than any other part of the church. It was ancient, apostolic, authentic, and catholic; therefore it was a model for those who desired continuity with the ancient church. Luther found himself in accord with substantive theological positions and practices of the Orthodox church, including use of the vernacular in the mass, rejection of private masses, reception of both bread and wine by the laity, freedom of the clergy to be married,[2] rejection of the doctrines of purgatory and of indulgences, and rejection of universal papal jurisdiction. In his 1519 debate with Eck, Luther invoked the position of "the Greek Church" to prove his point: all bishops are equally successors of the apostles; the Council of Nicaea accords to Rome only a primacy of honor, not of jurisdiction; the church fathers were not heretics just because they did not submit to papal primacy. The "Greek Orthodox" are "the most Christian people and the best followers of the Gospel on earth." He concluded that if there is one mother church of Christendom, it is ancient Orthodox Jerusalem, not Catholic Rome.

Philip Melanchthon, Luther's younger colleague, pursued Luther's concern to develop rapport with the Orthodox.

---

[2]The norm in Orthodoxy is a married (before ordination), family-based pastorate alongside celibate monastics.

Stymied by the inaccessibility of the Ecumenical Patriarchate, which had fallen under Turkish occupation, he turned towards Venice where many Orthodox scholars had fled to escape the Turks' occupation of Greek Orthodox Anatolia. There he contacted Antony the Exarch, a refugee from Corfu, indicating that he was eager for unity and hoping for Orthodox encouragement. In 1558 Orthodox Patriarch Joasaph II—distinguished, popular, scholarly—sent Deacon Demetrios Mysos, an elderly Montenegrin, to Wittenberg, Germany, to gather firsthand information about the Lutheran Reformation. Demetrios was well received by the Lutherans, became a close friend of Melanchthon's slavophile son-in-law, and was respected as a man of "exemplary piety and admirable morals." He stayed six months, and probably helped translate the Lutherans' Augsburg Confession into Greek. Returning to Constantinople he carried a copy of the Lutheran Confession to the patriarch with a covering letter from Melanchthon calling attention to those matters held in common by Lutherans and Orthodox: Scriptures, prophets, apostles, the Nicene Creed, dogmas of the seven Ecumenical Councils, and doctrines of the church fathers.

Patriarch Jeremias II succeeded Joasaph, and in 1573 initiated an extended exchange of correspondence with a group of Lutheran theologians in Tübingen, Germany. That correspondence has been well documented and well studied.[3] I commend it to the reader for careful study, but will limit my comments here to two. The correspondence began in the most irenic and promising spirit. If it had been held fifty or sixty years earlier the course of Reformation history would likely have been radically different. In the early 1500s Lutherans were in a formative period of discerning, reflecting, evaluating, and authenticating their beliefs. At the core of their faith was their experience of the Living Word *(viva vox evangelii)*. In some sense they were where the early Christians were prior to the first Ecumenical Council (Nicaea,

---

[3]See particularly Fr. G. Mastrantonis's excellent documentation and evaluation, *Augsburg and Constantinople* (Holy Cross Orthodox Press, Brookline, MA, 1982).

325 C.E.): a vibrant faith, an emerging body of belief and practice still to be articulated. The Lutherans were also openly concerned for a relationship with the Orthodox. But by 1573 the formative process had become crystallized. Erratic offshoots required correction or responsible direction. Beliefs were spelled out in "approved" statements: at Augsburg in 1530, and at Magdeburg in 1550. With the drafting and acceptance of the Formula of Concord (1577, adopted in 1580), Lutheran practice was fixed. Correctness was tested by the Formula, and became rigid, defensive, scholastic. That spirit transformed the promising exchange with the Orthodox from an open "win-win" conversation to a "win-lose" confrontation. The correspondence was broken off by the patriarch with an expressed hope of continued friendly communication, but no ongoing expectation of a common search for unity. Soon after the last reply of Patriarch Jeremias (1581), Lutheran King John III of Sweden addressed an appeal to the patriarch for "Christian reunion." It is not surprising that the patriarch did not reply.

If first frustrated by in-house problems of the Lutherans, the momentum towards union was further frustrated by Orthodox political necessities under Turkish occupation and by an unexpected development within Orthodoxy. Already in the Jeremias-Tübingen correspondence, the Tübingen Lutherans were suspected by the Orthodox of having "a regrettable taste for iconoclasm" (icon bashing). With the accession of Cyril Lukaris to the patriarchate, that misperception was further compounded. Lukaris's opponents, politically supported Roman Catholic clerics as well as fellow Orthodox, identified him as a "thief and a Lutheran ... he teaches in a manner that exceeds the limits (of Orthodox dogma), and he deceives the people." Here, we need deal only with the way Lutheranism was mistakenly involved.[4] Lukaris, before his election as Ecumenical Patriarch, was representative of the patriarchate in Poland, assisting the

---

[4]At the time of the Reformation, there was a great deal of confusion in both Roman Catholic and Orthodox areas about the various Reformation movements. For

Orthodox churches there in their resistance to (Roman) Uniate[5] takeover. When he became patriarch in 1620 he continued his distrust of Roman Catholics and hoped for help from the Protestant world against Turkish oppression of the Orthodox world. An energetic leader, intellectual and internationalist, he carried on correspondence with King Gustavus Adolphus of Sweden, and Prince Gabor of Transylvania; he also had connections with King James and Charles I of England, with the Archbishop of Canterbury, and with friends in Holland, Switzerland, and elsewhere. In 1629 Lukaris's *An Eastern Confession of the Christian Faith* was published in Geneva. In his article on justification Lukaris was indeed close to Lutherans: "justified by faith, not works (which are) testimonies of our faith and a confirmation of our calling ... (but) in no way adequate to save man." On iconoclasm, predestination, scriptural authority, baptism and Eucharist (which "faith receives spiritually"), points on which Lutherans contested against Calvinists, he was closer to Calvinism than to Lutherans. In any case, Orthodox theologians found him not Orthodox. Nor would Lutherans find him authentically Lutheran. What he attempted to do was to construct a synthesis of Eastern Orthodox dogma and Calvinist theology, blending the geniuses of both. In that, Lukaris satisfied no one, least of all his own church, which anathematized him as a heretic.

Later Developments
The 18th and 19th centuries brought the Great Awakening in America, Pietism throughout Britain and Europe, and the devel-

example, in the colonization of Florida, when French settlers established a colony at Fort Caroline near St. Augustine (1554–1565), Philip II of Spain sent Pedro Menendez to oust them. Menendez informed them that they were to be killed, not because they were French, but because they were "Lutheran heretics." They were in fact Calvinist Huguenots. The island where they were killed is named Matanzas (Place of Slaughter). J. P. Waterburg, ed., *The Oldest City: St. Augustine Saga of Survival* (St. Augustine Historical Society, St. Augustine, FL, 1983), Ch. 2.

[5]Uniates: Orthodox churches brought under the jurisdiction and doctrines of the Roman Catholic Church, usually by force, but permitted to keep their liturgical customs and married clergy, hence, "Eastern Rite Catholics" or "Uniates."

opment of aggressive programs of proselytizing directed at much of the Orthodox world. Lutherans were not major participants in that undertaking, but, particularly in their pietistic off-shoots, Lutherans were not clean-handed. In some cases missions were undertaken to convert "heathens" in "distant" lands (meaning mostly Muslims), and when that proved unproductive, programs of evangelism and proselytizing were directed towards Orthodox fellow believers. Not many were persuaded, and it is to the credit of Orthodox faithfulness that they were not. But it is a shameful mark on Protestantism (as on Rome's Uniatism two centuries earlier) that such enormous energies could be put towards an attack on Orthodoxy, and not on cooperation with Orthodoxy in her mission. A century later that practice was corrected, at least in part.

For the story of Lutheran-Orthodox contacts in early North America very little documentation is readily available (a good project for a research scholar). During the heroic years of Russian Orthodox mission work in Alaska and the American Northwest, there was virtually no Lutheran presence in the area. By the time Greek, Serbian, and other Orthodox immigrants arrived in sizeable numbers on the East Coast and in the north-central states, Lutherans were already settled into their own ethnic enclaves and took little notice, beyond cautious suspicion, of their new Orthodox neighbors. There were some instances of sharing. The church bell at the Orthodox Holy Ascension of Christ Church in Albion, Michigan, bears the inscription "The Salem Evangelical Lutheran Church," and in Minnesota neighboring Lutherans shared with Orthodox members in restoring an abandoned church for the Orthodox parish. While proselytizing activities were aimed at Orthodox faithful by some groups, there is virtually no evidence of intentional proselytizing between Orthodox and Lutherans except for mixed marriages.

With all the vicissitudes of our past relationships, mixed as they frequently were with the vagaries of the political world, there has been an enduring fascination with each other and with our Lord's call to unity, which has drawn us again and again into dialogue and common cause in the world. In the first half of the 20th century ecumenical concerns brought Orthodox and Lutheran leaders together for the creation of Faith and Order, Life and Work,[6] and eventually the World Council of Churches, for shared programs of postwar reconstruction and leadership training. Bilateral dialogues, including Greeks, Germans, Finns, Russians, and Rumanians, began in Europe in 1959, in India shortly thereafter, and in North America in 1968 where, from 1917 to 1950, emigres in large numbers had arrived from the Orthodox East and provided an extensive and representative Orthodox presence. We have now completed two rounds of official dialogue. The reports of the most recent round are available in print.[7] It is the author's hope that the personal "dialogues" that follow will supplement these scholarly reports with some colorful human interest and fresh perspectives on our similarities and dissimilarities. The time has come when we can all, Orthodox and Lutheran, be involved.

[6]These two predecessor movements leading to the creation of the World Council of Churches began in the late 1920s, Faith and Order dealing with matters of doctrine and church polity, Life and Work with ethics and social action.

[7]J. Meyendorff and R. Tobias, eds., *Salvation in Christ: A Lutheran-Orthodox Dialogue,* *Vol. I* (Augsburg Fortress Publishers, Minneapolis, MN, 1992); see Introduction, note 1, for information regarding Vol. II.

Promenading in Bulgaria, courtyard of Rila monastery

Boulevards and Village Squares

Sofia, Bulgaria, 1946. It was a balmy summer evening. My host, a young bishop of the Bulgarian Orthodox Church, and I decided on a walk before dinner. As we stepped out the door of the hotel, the great bells atop St. Alexander Nevsky Cathedral began their concert across the rooftops and tree-lined boulevards of the city. Even Marxists loved those bells, though they despised the liturgy going on below them. We paused a moment to listen, then another step and we were caught up in the human river flowing along the boulevard.

It's a delightful custom, this promenading. From about 5:30 to 8:00 each evening it seemed every family, all ages, enjoyed a promenade, up one street and down another, circling, milling, pausing to greet or chat or look in shop windows, more than half of which displayed works of art, music, hand-crafts, and books. No hurry. No bustle or shoving. No vehicular traffic, fumes, or noise except the soft shuffling of feet and the chatter of friendship.

What a contrast to Chicago! There, when a light turns green, you hope for the help of a traffic cop, or race across the street for your life. My host knew Chicago. I asked him how he explained the difference. He paused, then mused: "Maybe it's because we're already where we're going." Was that an answer, or a riddle for deeper reflection?

I remembered the small town in Kansas where I grew up—the county courthouse in the middle of "the square," surrounded by red-brick pop and mom stores, handling mostly basic necessities. On Saturday nights, farm chores and supper were finished early and everyone in the county came to town for weekly shopping. But that was the smallest part of it. Papa would give each of us a nickel for an ice cream cone, then from 7:00 'til 9:30 we, with all the rest, would promenade and visit around the square, stopping long enough to hear the boys' and men's band concerts once they had tuned up. It was like Sofia: "already where we're going."

A Promised Land?

But what did the bishop mean, really? That generation in Kansas was only pausing to catch its breath. The generation before and the next to come were on the move. Our forebears left where they were, mostly in northern Europe, to get to another land. Arriving on the East Coast of America, they soon moved on to another "other place"—to Pennsylvania, to Ohio, and Illinois, to the Midwest, and on to the West Coast. The farm boy leaves the farm for more exotic pursuits, the laborer becomes middle class, moves on to make his first half-million, but doesn't stop there. Busy church leaders interrupt one busy activity to get on to another meeting somewhere else, hurry through that agenda to leave early for something somewhere else. In much of Western Christendom, baptism, church membership, communion, and moral life are meant to ensure safe passage *from* where we are *to* another place where we assume we are not. And if it takes right theology, right administration of sacraments, right ministry, and right works for that passage, by all means believe, think, obey, establish, and do them, if that will get us to that "promised land" somewhere not yet reached. It is the compulsive drive of westerners: to get somewhere beyond where we are.

But it's not just that we are westerners, or work-ethic-driven Protestants. There is something in all of creation that senses its unfinishedness, that yearns for the security of a final "steady state," or promised land, or heaven, and seeks to find or construct that by moving beyond the present unfinished moment or place to another. It is as deep down as the place where time and measured space are being created out of configuration or Hilbert space, the shadowy pre-space not measured by yardsticks and watches, where quarks as the beginning of "things" are spun out of "no-thing" *(nihilo)* and scramble about for other quarks with which they can relate, begin their course, combine into hadrons, electrons, protons, atoms, etc., right up through the Comptean ladder to animals, planets, galaxies, and beyond. Call it "unfinished-ness," "incompleteness," "longing," "urge," "appetancy," "5th Constant,"[1] or "courage to be." Like original sin, from bottom up they (we) all have it. But we don't all exercise it the same way.

In the West, we have to be scientific, systematic, intentional about it. We go after whatever is lacking, with microscope, bulldozer, rocket, and bank roll—whatever gets us there faster. Though we're not quite sure what is lacking, we know we're not quite satisfied. And if we were? A middle-aged, upperclass housewife in the north suburbs said to me: "My husband has it made. He doesn't need me. My children are grown; they don't need me. I have no vocation, no purpose. So also most of my friends. Some try to drown their boredom in drinks or drugs. Some play bridge. Some find brief excite-ment with an affair. But all are still unsatisfied. I'm trying education and service." Busy-ness and "success" are still not "where we're going." Meaningful life is somewhere in the questing. But it is not all in the quest.

In Sofia—true, Americans don't usually think of Bulgaria as a peak civilization—but in Sofia, Orthodox Christians may

---

[1]5th Constant: The fifth of nine constants described by nuclear physicists as controlling factors in the formation of all created matter, the fifth being quark-to-quark attraction—in people language, the communalizing of likes, basic to all societal levels, including the human level. It also means incompleteness for entities in isolation.

have arrived at and dealt with the peak that historian Arnold Toynbee regards as essential to ascending civilizations: etherealization. That is, they have transfigured material achievements into spiritual, esthetic, creative, lasting qualities. The storefronts and promenaders already demonstrate that: arts, music, literature, learning, conversation, communality, wholeness. It is an ever-discovering, developing, enlarging network of relationships—relating all, in the sense of "field theory," to all through all time and everywhere. And that is a tremendously exciting place to be; where one doesn't "leave thy low-vaulted past," nor is one "shut from heaven with a dome more vast,"[2] but knows the present reality of both, and of being free, even under Communist tyranny. Unlike that proverbial chicken that had to scurry across the road "to get to the other side," for that great family of Orthodox Christians in East Europe, the "other side" is already here. They don't have to dash hither and yon to find it. In gentle companionship they celebrate it, with all, everywhere, forever.

Remembering Pioneer Communities
Our annual family reunions in Kansas were wondrous occasions, especially for us kids. After church on Sunday everyone hurried to the park, all the respected uncles and aunts and grandparents—respected preferably at a distance—and fiancees to be teased, and cousins with pony-tails to be pulled. Mothers set out three times as much food as we could eat, with every kind of salad, vegetable, meat, and other delicacies still too exotic to appear in cookbooks, like shoo-fly pie and home-cranked real ice *cream*. There was always a designated pray-er, slightly less prankish than the rest, after which the call was "kids first." Eating finished, there were swings and slides for the little ones, rope jumping contests, darebase and ball games for the teenagers, croquet and horseshoes for the men, plus visiting and catching up on gossip all around. At the end of the afternoon, the mothers

---

[2]From stanza five of Oliver Wendell Holmes's poem "The Chambered Nautilus."

again set out the food on the picnic tables and we stuffed ourselves again. It was a full day's event, richly rewarding and memorable.

Besides reunions and Saturday night promenading, there were also the monthly "literary society" meetings on Friday night at the country school. There were skits, readings, poetry recitations, solos and duets and choruses, and collections for worthy causes such as neighbors who had been burned out. And then there were pies and cakes, and tag surreptitiously played around the dark school yard. The whole community came. Anyone absent meant someone should see who was sick or what else was wrong.

That was almost two generations ago. The last family reunion we got to was at the local church youth camp. Families came as always right after church, or after golf. Mothers emptied their food baskets onto the tables, more reasonably scaled down from the proud efforts of their grandmothers. We ate, chatted over our food, packed up the leftovers, and everyone left, all going their separate ways, in a hurry to get "somewhere else." Why? I'm not sure. Was it to avoid getting too close, too involved, too uncomfortable with deeper conversation and sharing? In any case, "re-union," like the Old Settlers' Picnics that seem to have run their course, was not "where we're going." We want to get "somewhere else" and quickly, not quite realizing that we'll have to slow down, even to *see* the roses.

While in Europe, my wife Trudy and I were driving through a part of Serbia where we wanted to check out the aftermath of World War II destruction and postwar assistance to the Orthodox churches. It was late afternoon as we approached a small village. Down in the meadow was a circle of twenty or thirty young people, arms locked across shoulders, dancing the kolo. I have forgotten with what musical instruments— probably a double wooden flute, a stringed guzla, some kind of drum improvised with sticks and a hollow log. We had

13

seen East European folk dancers in New York, in Moscow, and in Paris. They were great entertainers, whether on stage or at restaurants. But why out here in the country, after a day's hard work, and for whom? There were no spectators, except the cows and us. Why, then? Obviously, for the joy of it. They were celebrating the day, the cool grass, the sky, life, creation, and one another—for the joy of it. So, like our Native American friends at their powwows—a spiritual dance, celebrating the Great Spirit, the whole creation, and one another—not to get somewhere else. So, Pythagoras, here are your earthly *armonias,* and God's, where the pulse of the stars, the beat of the heart, the rhythm of neutrons and protons, the meter of music, the measure of space and time and sound, your "music of the spheres," meet in the joy of these sensitive souls in harmony and participation with all the rest.

Promenading Western Style
Our shopping mall is okay for promenading, at least in winter. It's open an hour before shoppers arrive. No snow, rain, cold, or mud, and it meets the doctor's orders: three miles a day to keep cholesterol down and heart beat up. But it's a lonely place. Two hundred of us are present there, but not present to one another. We don't really see each other— just each other's backs, or backsides.

It reminds me of my childhood, driving a team of horses on a cultivator. Except when turning corners, one saw only the horses' bouncing butts. A graduate student of mine was concerned that that was what was happening at his church every Sunday morning. Families arrived by car at the curb, got out, walked down the sidewalk, up the steps, into the foyer, down the aisle, into the pew, knelt to pray, and stood to sing. And what did they see? Each other's backs. After the benediction, the procedure was reversed. What did they see? The backs of those they missed coming in. So this student rearranged the foyer, the entrance, and the seating so people had to mill around, see each other face to face. Sofia!

Kolo dancing

And at the mall, we're not all oldies on surgical "rehab" anymore. There are some young mothers with babies, some who are younger or middle-aged, and frequently I pass small clusters of lively ones sauntering gracefully around the course, engaged in animated conversation that often sounds to me like Greek or Russian or something else out of that special world of Eastern Orthodoxy. But we still have to look to see each other.

I walk at the mall to get it over with—fast. It's like shopping. I know what I need to get, get it, get it over with, and get back to my project. Trudy, my wife, on the other hand, lingers, especially when around handcrafts, those lovely things from another human's effort, even more especially the most simple and primitive. It's as though this object is some kind of bond between her and its creator. They almost talk to, or touch one another through this or that object, as with a good piece of sculpture. Who can resist reaching out to caress good sculpture, the "hand" of the sculptor?

Icons? Moments of contact, talking, touching, promenading together—the joys of endless familial wholeness. Is heaven only above? Or is it the deeper dimensions of here? Here and now. Already where we're going.

Churchyards and Battlefields

Near Zica, Yugoslavia, I was driving the editor of an American religious journal to several Orthodox church sites where we had shared in postwar reconstruction. During lunch with Orthodox Bishop German, later Patriarch German, my editor friend asked for some statistics: "How many members do you have in your diocese, Bishop?" "About 200,000," he replied. The editor looked across the valley to the encircling hills. "Surely there's some mistake. There can't be more than 10,000 people in those villages and farms." The bishop smiled, "Ah, yes. But you asked about 'members,' not about 'people.' This is the valley of Kosovo, where 100,000 Serbian Christians died in the late 14th century defending the country against invading Turks. They are all members of my diocese." Plus a good many others who have died, though not "departed," since. They are all present and participate with the "living" in the liturgy and spiritual life of the Serbian Orthodox Church.

In 1955 Ecumenical Patriarch Athenagoras requested the World Council of Churches to send a fact-finding team to Istanbul, Turkey. Riots, allegedly sparked by Turkish students, had broken out throughout the city, against the small community of Greek Orthodox Christians still there after centuries of Turkish Muslim oppression. It was our task to help locate the origins and reasons for the riots, to enquire about appropriate assistance, and to report back to concerned international agencies. One clear finding of our investigation was that the rioters had not so much targeted living Greek Christians with their fury as they had the tombs and remains of the dead. To the Orthodox that was devastating, not just as a measure of desecration and disrespect, but as seriously interfering with the repose, the presencing, and the bodily resurrection of the deceased. For them, the living and the dead are still inseparably bound in a shared life and a common, living destiny.

American Indians, I am told, have some quite similar percep- tions. Not only is the Great Spirit immanently involved with the spirits of the "living" and the "dead," but the spirits of the "dead" are so inextricably participants with their material bodies and with the living, that they are not fully released (resurrected?) until flesh has finally returned to earth, to ashes, to dust. Indian care for burial places therefore has far more significance than the prolonging of good memories and respect. It's a participation in earth and "heaven."

How different is it with American Lutherans? Fisherville, pronounced "Visherwille" in Pennsylvania Dutch, is a village of perhaps ten families situated in a broad valley between two mountain ranges in central Pennsylvania. In the middle of the village, at the top of the hill, stands a small Lutheran church. Surrounding the church is a fenced churchyard with all sorts of grave markers, including those of my forebears going back as far as three hundred-plus years. Unlike many modern cities that quickly disown their dead by burying them out in the country or across the tracks, Fisherville is glad to have its deceased kin close at hand. I'm much moved by worship there. As a boy I found it a bit spooky to have to walk past the gravestones to get to the church door ("step a little faster, please"). Sometimes it even seemed like the "spooks" came right along with us into church. Now I delight also in that and find it warmly gratifying to walk among the graves before entering for worship. And when in

St. Peter's Lutheran Church and churchyard, Fisherville, Pennsylvania. In Orthodoxy, cemeteries are regarded as continuations or extensions of the church.

the liturgy we come to the preface to the Eucharist—
"Therefore with angels and archangels and with all the company of heaven we laud and magnify Thy glorious name ..."—I know that there are indeed more presences there than those of us holding down the pews. I'm grateful not only for what that whole company has provided for us, but that they are there and host us.

There's a moving scene near the end of Thornton Wilder's play, *Our Town,* in which the inhabitants of the cemetery are in veiled communication about (with?) the present inhabitants of "our town." Does that seem strange? In our home town, Racine, Wisconsin, the Greek Orthodox Church has the usual family of icons dividing the altar area from the main sanctuary: Christ the Savior, Mary and Child, John the Baptist, and angels, with Mary Theotokos above the altar and a huge Pantokrator (all-powerful) Christ in the dome. The stained glass windows in the north and south walls, nearly a score of them, depict apostles and well-known saints. Another Orthodox church, St. Sava Serbian Cathedral in Milwaukee, Wisconsin, is a Western masterpiece patterned inside after the great 6th century St. Sofia Cathedral in Constantinople (Istanbul). The interior walls are entirely covered with resplendent mosaics of saints, prophets, the heavenly hosts, and signal events in our Hebrew-Christian tradition. In the original St. Sofia, restorationists are slowly peeling off the paint and plaster laid on by devout Muslim occupiers to cover the ancient Christian mosaics. Every visit I find more moving than the last, to stand in the presence of these magnificent icons. Little wonder that the emissaries sent by Russian Prince Vladimir more than a thousand years ago, to check out whether this Christian religion was something they should adopt in Russia, were so deeply impressed. On returning to Russia, they reported to their prince that it was all so glorious they didn't know whether they were on earth or already in heaven!

These icons, in St. Sofia, or St. Sava, or Racine's Kimissis Theotokou, or in Orthodox homes, perhaps also in Indian totems, are not there as great works of art—though even Marxists recognized that they were that—nor yet as visual aids for instruction. In and through them the whole company—prophets, apostles, martyrs—the whole company of heaven, past and future, are present. Respectfully, one greets those closest with a prayer candle or a kiss of peace and affection. Strange? What young swain hasn't kissed the picture of his beloved, or what widow the symbols of her beloved departed? They are somehow present. Even Karl Barth, famous Swiss theologian who could hardly be considered a mushy sentimentalist, used to say that when he had an issue with St. Paul—and he had several—he took Paul's texts and sat down at his desk with St. Paul, and they went at it. Paul was present to him through the Scriptures, but even a bit more than that.

The Action of the Whole Church
In the Orthodox Divine Liturgy, whose common origins with the Lutheran liturgy trace back through St. John Chrysostom in the 4th century, the beginning part of the service (*enarxis*— beginning, and *synaxis*—meeting) is as much convocation of the whole church universal as it is invocation to God to be present. With the words, "Again and again," the worship leader convokes the congregation of believers *and saints* to be present. Indeed, one of the longer prayers is like a detailed roll call, beginning, by name, with the archangels, and continuing through the prophets, the apostles, the hierarchs, the martyrs, the church fathers and mothers, wonderworkers, ancestors, liturgists, patriarchs and bishops, priests and monks, the departed and living faithful. Likewise, in the preparation of the bread for the Eucharist, the several parts of the *prosphoron* (leavened loaf) signal the gathering together of the entire church of God: Christ the head, Mary Theotokos, and all members of the Body, past, present, and future. The liturgy itself is then the action of the whole church—militant and triumphant—and the Eucharist is celebrated "on behalf of all and for all," never really quite ending.

Why prayer candles in the liturgy, in our homes, in festive celebrations? There's something fascinating about candle-light, about a fireplace, about matches—to all ages. It's more than the light, the flickering, the risk, the warmth. There's something living about it. In pre-Christian Scandinavia, our Swedish ancestors carried lighted candles through the burial grounds to awaken the deceased and escort them into the temples in the darkness of winter—the *levande ljus*—lighted candles that enliven again our nearness to the departed, and still evident in Scandinavian Christmas customs. At our

21

family meals we always have a lighted candle. I asked Trudy how she explained that. "Well, it's cheery on a grey day. It's cozy. It's alive." But more than that, it means that we are all gathered, let the celebration begin! I glance across the room at an enlarged photograph of our youngest boy killed in a school bus accident, alongside an icon of St. Nicholas. As our youngest daughter says, there's always an empty place at our family table—no Philip. But Philip and St. Nicholas are both there anyway. Merely a burning candle? Earth, air, fire, and water—the whole creation, the company of heaven is there.

Past. Present. Future. Is time really so discretely segmented? In Western dichotomous modes of thinking, we construct "wholeness" by combining parts into totals. I suppose Aristotle taught us that, also to dig out the meaning of reality by dissecting and examining discrete parts, piece by piece, with microscopic finesse. Eastern thought and life is whole by inter-relation and integration. Not only are the "dead"—the saints, the martyrs, the loved ones—not far removed from community with the "living," but the holy and the earthy, the so-called "present" and the "future," the "here" and "here-after," are mutually participant in each other. In our family collection is a copy of the *panagioi* (all saints) icon. It's a framed icon almost entirely of heads—Christ in the center surrounded by apostles, martyrs, prophets, evangelists, patriarchs, and saints of every age and nation—an icon jammed full of the heads of saints. Yet there is more. All around the frame is a row of open figure sixes. It took a medical student to explain that to me: the figure six is the symbol for the yet unborn. And they are all part of the living church.

The holy and the earthy—are they worlds apart? To be saints does not mean to be non-earthy. To be God does not mean to be non-earthy. That was the issue running through all seven of the Ecumenical Councils: Is it possible for Holy God to take on earthiness without losing his godness? The church affirmed against all kinds of would-be protectors of God's pure holiness, from Mani and Arius to Bogomils and iconoclasts, that God *could* take earthy form and still be God. He could and he did. And the unequivocal accent given to incarnational Christology in the creeds, as well as the place ascribed very early to Mary as historical, earthy mother and bearer of God *(Theotokos)*, is substantial evidence of Orthodoxy's determination to counter the Hellenistic, Muslim, and sometimes Jewish ideas that God could only be God if he kept his robes unsoiled by earthiness. What *good* news would it have been if they, the Orthodox, had lost? No incarnation. No God-among-us. And so far as I can see, Orthodoxy is still doing that as against all manner of would-be "God-protectors": pietists, radical Calvinists, puritans, iconoclasts, and other-worldly cults. Orthodoxy, and correct Lutheranism, affirm still the appropriateness of earthy senses in liturgical life: smell, taste, sound, touch, sight—incense, candles, icons, music, bread and wine, wheat *(kollyva)*—the whole creation gathered with the saints, bearers of divine manifestations.

So what is liturgy? Not just another thing the church does. It is what the church is—a cosmic family reunion, perpetually gathered around a mystery and sharing it, conversing, listening, glorifying and thanking the Triune God, and feasting again with him. It encompasses a sanctuary, the churchyard, the battlefield—all—"already where we're going."

Icons and Ornaments

Fifty miles west of Corinth our small party was to leave the army-guarded highway and climb up through the gorge to Kalavryta monastery. It was the late 1940s. Greece was under siege. The Nazi and Fascist foreigners had been driven out, leaving all but the largest Greek cities devastated. But now an internal civil war between the Andartes (Greek rebels assisted by Communists from the north) and Greek loyalists was strangling the whole country. The hills and forests were controlled by the rebels. Villagers fled into larger towns, ringed by barbed-wire hung with grenades and mines and guarded by troops with rifles. Safe travel was possible only by military convoy.

Our only access to Kalavryta for international relief was by narrow-gauge cog train. Prof. Hamilcar Alivisatos, representing the Greek archbishop, Judy Gaselee, representing the British Council of Churches, and I climbed aboard a tiny boxcar sixteen feet long pulled by a very small cog engine. The minister of education from Athens and the local Orthodox bishop joined us as we started up the narrow gorge, which cut a gash upward through the mountains. Armed guards were positioned at the open car doors and on the engine. One of the guards explained that a few days before they had been ambushed by rebels in the gorge and that one of the train crew had been killed. At the top of the

24

gorge was a broad valley, a veritable Shangri-la, nestled among the mountains. Professor Alivisatos pointed to the monastery on the cliff across the valley. It had been burned out by the Nazis after they had shot six of the monks and thrown fifteen others over the precipice. In 1821 it was from a tree above this monastery that Greek Archbishop Germanos had flown an icon banner portraying the angel's annunciation to the Virgin Mary to signal the beginning of what was to become the Greeks' victorious war of independence against the Turks.

As we approached the valley's hillside town, the bishop prepared us for the people we would meet. At one time the town comprised two thousand people, mostly farmers and vintners. During World War II Greek fighters in the mountains had attacked a Nazi outpost in the town and fled. As a reprisal the Nazis gathered all the people one night in front of the school. The women and children, with ten of the oldest men, were driven into the school building, which was then set on fire. Immediately, the Nazis went from house to house and burned every building that would burn. The men and boys were led out into the hills. Fortunately, an Austrian officer was quite sympathetic with the people. Stealing around to the back door of the school, he unlocked it and let the women and children escape into the woods. The women started searching for their husbands and sons, and found them on a slope above the town, twelve hundred of them massacred and eleven hardly living. With unbelievable courage the women and children buried their loved ones, then began rebuilding with their bare hands, first their church, which had been burned out, then their homes, gardens, and fields.

We joined the women and children in a procession up the hill to the sacred burial ground of their husbands, fathers, and sons, to lay a wreath and say some words of comfort, appreciation, and hope concerning the village and the future. The women in black soon went off, each to the graves of her

25

loved ones. As we came back down to the valley we could look again towards the hill and see it speckled with black where the women lovingly tended the graves and sprinkled the earth with their tears. Sporadic, unfriendly rebel rifle fire could be heard in the surrounding hills.

At the monastery there was much sharing of war stories and of future hopes. A new cornerstone was laid and the foundation for a new building was started by the bishop. After a delicious afternoon dinner—we must get back down the gorge before dark—the monastery community, gracious hosts that they were, presented me with an ancient Byzantine icon of the *Theotokos* (Madonna and Child). It is a "wounded" Mary. Prior to independence, Turkish occupiers had stripped the icon of its silver frame, also the silver halo above Mary, and had stabbed the cheek of Mary with a bayonet. This was not the first, nor will it be the last image of the Holy wounded by icon smashers (iconoclasts).

In the highlands of south-central Turkey, just north of the Taurus mountains, early Christians lived in caves hewn into the cliffs and cones of soft volcanic rock. The walls and ceilings of these homes and chapels they painted with Christian icons. The area (Cappadocia) is largely abandoned now, Christians having been driven out by Turkish conquerors a thousand years ago. When I visited there recently, I was deeply impressed by the simple design and soft colors of the frescoed icons and the persons represented. But, of several hundred observed, all had been speared in the face— wounded saints—with bayonets or some other sharp instruments, presumably by Muslims or other iconoclasts. Today, the Turkish government regards the area as a vast museum, provides limited protection from vandals, and is seeking assistance for preservation and restoration.

Sixth century St. Sofia in Istanbul, already mentioned in Chapter 2, with a floor area the size of a football field, was so resplendent with its mosaic icons that the emissaries of Prince

An iconoclast shooting at the icon of St. George; Russian
Museum, St. Petersburg, early 16th century, adapted.

Vladimir of Russia who were not yet Christian exclaimed that being there was "already to be in heaven!" Not, however, for the Turkish Muslim conquerors. To them, icons were blasphemy. The Divine God is spirit, spirit only, and should not be represented in human form. So they plastered over the entire interior, then painted it with abstract designs and Arabic script. Today, the Turkish government officially takes a neutral attitude to such religious representations and has allowed the gradual cleaning of the plaster from the ancient mosaics. I find being in such grandeur again "almost to be in heaven." Across the garden from St. Sofia, the great Muslim Blue Mosque magnificently portrays what simple abstract art can mean to the human spirit—but it is not the same meaning.

The Cathedral of St. Pierre in Geneva, Switzerland, when it was still Roman Catholic, had great stained glass windows, statuary, stations of the cross, and other visual images and icons in Roman Catholic style. When the pre-Calvinist reformation took over, all of that was threatened with destruction, and was cleared out of the cathedral. Today, one would have to say that the Cathedral, in its Calvinist austerity, seems "bare," empty, and cold. Fortunately, the stained glass windows were secretly stolen away, "buried" for years, and now can be seen in a Geneva museum— "displaced saints," waiting to be restored to their proper places in the cathedral when the time comes. The cathedral in Lyon, France, and many others did not fare so well. Calvinist iconoclasts not only removed the interior icons of various kinds, but also knocked off the heads of the architectural statuary in the entrance arches, windows, and spires. Similarly for a thousand years, from the 6th to the 17th century, religious history is strewn with these and other unspeakable atrocities against icons and the defenders of icons (iconodules).

What was going on here? In the ecumenical spirit of the day it's not polite to criticize, but we cannot ignore some serious differences. For Jews, though they did have some images of

28

their own, it was forbidden to make graven images such as were found among their pagan neighbors (Exodus 20:4, Deut. 5:8). Why? God is a spirit; him we do not see. No one will *see* God and live. Further, to claim that the unseeable God became a man was blasphemy. Here, there was a kinship between Judaism and Islam, and some evidences of collusion in smashing the icons of early Christians. Later Protestant iconoclasts, observing the fervent piety of Roman Catholics (kissing icons and statuary, kneeling and praying to Mary and the saints) and not distinguishing between respect or veneration *(proskynesis)* and worship *(latreia),* also saw this as idolatry. The "idols" had to go, for the sake of true spiritual communion with God. These "puritans" were of course in a long line of Christian purifiers, not just from the Old Testament: 5th century Paulicians of Samosata in Armenia, Bogomils in Bulgaria and Serbia, Catharii in north Italy, Albigensis in south France, Waldenses in the Italian Piedmont, Beghards and Beguines in northwest Europe, Calvinist Huguenots in central France and Switzerland, and Puritans and Quakers in America. The intention of virtually all iconoclasts has been to strip the faith to a purer, less of-the-flesh spirituality and to cleanse the temples of presumed idolatry. And to see them replaced—with what? Jews and Muslims employed abstract, "spiritualized" art forms, or flowers, birds, animals, landscapes, but not people. Calvinists in general and other puritans, after a period of austere temple cleansing, now "decorate" their religion with abstract colored glass and photographic style art—not considered idolatrous. Marxists believed they had their superstition-free faith in "pure science." Probably the most dramatic icon-smashing measures that I have experienced were in East Europe in the late 1940s—when young Marxists mocked and desecrated the elements of the Eucharist and baptism, and I could only stand silently by. Fortunately, their Marxist elders regarded icons as important works of art and gathered thousands of icons from churches, placing them in museums to "preserve" them—which they have done. To put the most charitable reading on their reasons for that: they wanted to free the "real," scientific world from superstition. And one way of doing that was, as for iconoclasts everywhere, to remove what believers regarded as sacred objects and the saints they represented from the possibilities of reverence and participation. American Indians face the same kind of problem when their symbols, sacred rites, and personhood are trashed and desecrated as sports mascots and smart advertising. Though their icon-smashers haven't thought out quite so clearly what they are doing, it has the same effect and must be corrected. Wounded God-bearers.

Could God Take Earthly Form?

What is at stake here? The last great Ecumenical Council of the undivided church (Nicaea, 787 C.E.) addressed that question—not merely the question of alleged idolatry, but whether God could take earthly form and remain God. The transcendent God's "purity" and the Incarnation were therefore at stake, and, related to that, whether nature and matter were opposed to spirit and faith, absolutely and irretrievably. The whole Trinity was therefore at stake. The council affirmed unequivocally not only that God became *man,* but that it was *God* who became man. Invisible God became visible man, and in doing so God made known that not only man, but God's whole creation is capable of manifesting, of "bearing" God *(Theotokos).* That does not mean that God equals creation (pantheism) nor that God equals all humankind, but that God is in, with, and under all creation (pan-en-theism).[1] Just as Mary does not *equal* God, but is capable of *bearing* God, so also an icon of earthy material, such as of St. Nicholas, does not equal but is capable of bearing, of participating in, of re-presenting St. Nicholas.

Iconographers are careful at this point not to equate icons with the historicity of persons. They do that in part by their artistic style. Avoiding sensual, emotional, body-builder or

---

[1]Panentheism *(pan-en-Theos)* accurately translated is "all in God." The corollary of that, *Theos-en-panta* ("God in all") means that all of creation has its ground of being in and of God—therefore, panentheism.

30

body-famished action-events, or Dorian Gray details, they portray the subject stylized, with a minimum of detail, face on (profile would imply turning away from the viewer). In short, in the icon we confront the person, as though transfigured, ready to converse with the viewer. Early icon smashers assumed that an icon, being of the same nature as what it represents, must be of the same substance and therefore essentially identical; thus an icon becomes an idol in representing, for example, Christ's human nature or his divine nature. Orthodox iconographers maintained that icons did not represent the nature, but the person of the one represented, that an icon of Christ was not an image of his divine nature but of his divine person incarnate, visible, a concrete person: "an icon is connected with its prototype not by being identical, but by portraying his person," which makes communion with that person possible. So Incarnation (as visibility of the invisible, tangibility) not only makes icons as re-presentational art possible, but also as necessary for the sake of incarnational extension and its cosmic consequences. As against the separation and desacralization of matter and spirit, icons reflect the conjoining of the earthly and heavenly, the Kingdom of God on earth, the transfiguration also of creation.

Functionally, icons do through our seeing what Scripture (the Word) does through our hearing. St. John Chrysostom reminds us that it is not an either/or matter: the Word is both visible and audible. There are, of course, possibilities of idolatry with both, particularly if the evident object is *equated* with the deeper reality within it. We observe, in passing, that the Western Reformation has had a primary concern with hearing (*Logos*, Word), while Eastern Christendom makes a larger place for seeing (*Phos*, Light; *Doxa*, Glory). That is doubtless related to different accents in salvation (to be examined later), but also a few hundred years ago it was related to the invention of the printing press and the immediate availability of the scriptural Word (audibility) to the masses in the West. Visibility through icons was still the prominent mode of mass communication in the East.

The American Culture

How is it now with Lutherans in North America? Lutheran immigrants to America did not set out to be icon smashers. Ironically, they just had some more pressing earthy priorities. Their mother churches in Scandinavia and north Europe had rejected the iconoclasm of the more radical Calvinist reformers. These Lutherans held onto material manifestations of divine epiphanies: icons, stained glass, organs, candles, statuary, grand cathedrals. And Luther, though not quite the mentor to Scandinavians that he was to Germans, maintained that it was quite correct to have icons, so long as they were not worshipped. Not surprising, perhaps, that when my family and I returned to America after some years of work and worship in European churches, we felt upon re-entering American Protestant churches (Lutherans less than others) as if we were entering empty, sterilized, bare, depersonalized halls. There was very little "messy human stuff" around, like incense, prayer candles, kissable icons, or mysterious shadows behind the altar. Just flat, characterless "realism."

Why this change in America from our Lutheran heritage? Scandinavian immigrants to America did indeed bring along their disillusionment with the "despotism" and "high church-iness" of their state churches. Beyond this, they arrived as literate but quite poor people, mostly farmers and menial laborers. Everything they gained in their first years here had to go towards survival on the frontier. There were no religious luxuries, no organs, no stained glass—a simple wooden chapel with *a capella* choirs would have to do. The main "symbols" were bare wooden crosses, a plain goblet for the Eucharist, and a kitchen pan for baptisms. Eventually pastors, communion and baptismal vessels, and musical instruments were added, but churchly architecture and other worship materials lagged until improved economic conditions and the liturgical renewal of the mid-1900s made "enrichments" possible. Our forebears were not intentionally icon smashers; they just couldn't afford iconic representations.

As time went on, another factor also contributed to a kind of passive iconoclasm among Lutherans, namely, the austere puritan rub-off of a predominantly Calvinist culture religion, combined with the flat sterility of modern glass and aluminum architecture. I cite an example from our recent parish. The sanctuary was originally designed to continue some of our Swedish heritage: a semicircular altar rail where the faithful knelt, completed by a half-arc altar and reredos representing God's presence in the churchly circle, with a hidden "mystery area" between the reredos and the wall, and a statue of Jesus above the altar blessing the communicants. Now, conforming to recent culture religion and slick modernization the statue has been removed to the stairwell. There is no reredos, no "mystery area"—just a flat brick wall and an altar redone "in the round" (actually squared), with a sterile, gloss-varnished, bare oak cross suspended from the ceiling— similar to hundreds of others I have seen in Methodist, Presbyterian, Baptist, and other nonliturgical churches across the land. It suggests that God is immaculately above—"spiritual"— not "in, with, and under." It is a strange theological-liturgical statement in a Lutheran church.

When of late in this culture we turned our eyes to divine epiphanies, we perceived only two-dimensionality, not great depth. Perhaps that was provisionally inevitable in a culture dominated by two-dimensional television, movies, billboards, cameras, sports events, etc. What you see is not only what you get. What you see with your eyes is all there is. Passive icon smashing of deeper realities has not and probably never will be eliminated from this culture, at least not as long as our love for the expendable "things" of God's creation is worlds apart from our love of deeper communion, and as long as dualism defines the nonrelationship between matter and spirit. Even the most traditional Orthodox and Lutherans can be infected with it. But there are promising signs. There's a hopeful serendipity in the fascination we have with "things" and visuals. Just as behind words is the Word is God, perhaps fascination with visuals could help us see that behind visuals is *Phos* (Light) is God. As a participant in the first round of Lutheran-Orthodox dialogue in North America observed, this (increase in visualization) has accelerated a change in our perception of the world by giving precedence of the visual over the verbal—to *see* more deeply. As I sit at this computer, finding icons on the screen, opening windows, discovering vast worlds of activity and inter-relationships behind them, it's a helpful analogy for understanding and entertaining the world of religious icons and presences. Further, it is encouraging to see that some Lutherans, now financially able to have more than empty halls for worship, and free in principle to restore our original iconic heritage and spiritual grounding are doing just that. More than superficial adornment, such action appears to rejoin the realm of spirit-matter and incarnational reality, which is genuine iconography.

The Liturgy and the Clock

The funeral for Orthodox Patriarch Gavrilo in Belgrade, May 1950, was a very moving experience, a glorious celebration of this courageous and beloved shepherd's victory. During World War II the Nazis locked him in the infamous Dachau concentration camp. After the war, even Communist President Tito pleaded with him to return to Yugoslavia for the sake of the people and future reconstruction, and personally gave him a private limousine so he could visit his parishes. At his funeral thousands were in attendance, including several thousand standing in the rain outside. It went on for four hours. Yes, four hours, standing! Unaccustomed as we were to standing in church, I think the Communist government's representative was if anything even more uncomfortable than I long before the liturgy ended. But we were determined to maintain respectful poise for His Holiness and his people. Many Orthodox believers seemed less constrained about our idea of propriety, entering at any time in the service, greeting and kissing one another and the coffin and icons, lighting and placing prayer candles at the iconostasis, leaving and returning at will.

Visiting Orthodox worship in many parts of the world, I was at first struck by the way people drifted casually in and out of the service. Let's say the service is announced for 9:00 a.m. Prior to that the priest and assistants have prepared themselves, the sanctuary, the altar, the bread and wine, with much prayer and incense, for the eucharistic liturgy. By 9:15 a handful of people including the lay reader and worship assistants are in place. The service proceeds with frequent return to the prayers—"Again and again let us pray for …" Impatient westerner that I am, I thought "For God's sake, why don't the people get here on time so the service can begin?" Arriving at any and all moments, Orthodox ease into it. For them there is no sharp break between nonliturgy and liturgy. The clock is not lord of that kind of time. Whenever all are gathered together—Holy Trinity, saints, martyrs, living and "dead"—the liturgy begins. That can mean about any time. They are always gathered; they were never un–gathered. To be "late" or absent from bits and parts of the liturgy by the clock does not mean to be not present. More than a begin-now-end-then recapitulation of the drama of incarnation, the liturgy is an unbroken continuum of that unceasing event. Those "arriving" pick up the ongoing conversation, the celebration, the thanksgiving, the event itself having in reality never stopped. And it is their privilege, those pulsing warm blood, to set the table for a far vaster company than is contained by walls, pews, and clocks. Not as though they were starting all over again, or repeating a last supper, or remaking a sacrifice from the past, but continuing it, participating forward and backward across time, in the same extended family event.

In such a continuous community of listening, telling, remembering, and rejoicing, the liturgy assuredly is not primarily a matter of instruction, certainly not entertainment, and neither needs nor can tolerate any dressing up calculated to attract crowds. Nor is its primary focus, humanly speaking (perhaps God has another focus), on the claims of individuals for their subjective hurts. Praying, in Western modes, is frequently a matter of informing God about what is the real situation here, as if he didn't know or needs a little arm-twisting to do something about it. With that perception, plus an assumption of infinite distancing between here and hereafter, one can

Participating in eternity at the funeral of Orthodox Patriarch Gavrilo. Many candles—no clocks.

understand why many faithful Protestants have reservations about what they assume are pleas by Orthodox faithful addressed *to* the saints, *to* Mary and to others who have "passed on" to an eternal abode. But if, on the other hand, these too, in the presence of the Holy Trinity, are also present in the liturgy, then prayers *with* them become more of a conversation taking place at the cosmic family reunion than plea bargaining by Local Saints' Union #777. The whole family is gathered—across time, space, cultures, languages, races, and sexes—communing together. What a reunion!

An Eschatological Perception
Ecumenical discussions have demonstrated how difficult it is to bridge between linear and eschatological views of history. By linear view, an event begins, happens, and ends. Then

another event begins, happens, and ends. By eschatological view, every event is part of all other events, not just discretely following one after another, like minutes of a clock. With such an eschatological or holistic understanding of time, Orthodox transcend several Western eucharistic problems: was Jesus' sacrifice unfinished? Incomplete the first time? Repeated with every Eucharist? Is there one sacrifice or are there many? From an eschatological standpoint, eucharistic sacrifice is not a clock question. What "happened" on Calvary is a forever happening of God. His love, his passion, his sacrifice is not an event that merely started and then ended at 3:00 on a Friday afternoon, 30 C.E., outside Jerusalem. It is the perpetual love and suffering of God for his creation, as much happening, as much really here in our midst today as ever. Across time, we had and we have our part in his betrayal and death. *Anamnesis* (usually translated "in remembrance," better translated "not forgetting") means not forgetting, returning there, prehending (grasping), confessing, celebrating. Of course the sacrifice is real. It never stopped. Nor does it need to be re-started. As the priest prays immediately prior to communing, "The Lamb of God ... is always fed upon and never consumed ..."

Similarly, from recognition of the perduring[1] presence of God as the Real in all reality, and from an eschatological perception of history that is able to recognize each moment as related to and encompassing all moments, *anamnesis* is not to recall Jesus forward to our presence—he is already present—but to call us to the *realization* of his presence, real and substantial in the very elements around us, some of which are particularly consecrated for a reminder and celebration of that fact, while momentarily curtaining out others. If in the Eucharist we have experienced the presence of God, the God who is not a distant spirit, but who has also become flesh and in becoming flesh from the beginning, *en arche* (John 1:1), is still present "in, with, and under" all reality, then our descriptions might note that what is really real and most really

---

[1]*Enduring:* extension in time; *perduring:* extension in both time and space.

present to us is not the molecular substance, but God-in-Christ in that substance, really present to our perception in the bread and wine, that is, Real Presence. As to how that happens, Orthodox colleagues appear to have very little concern with the "hocus pocus" questions—how, what, when—but far more concern to celebrate the *fact* of Real Presence. The more appropriate human question, the late Father Schmemann[2] reminds us in an unpublished paper, is not "what happens to the elements, how and when exactly does it happen? For the early church the real question was: what happens *to the church* in the Eucharist? ...The whole liturgical action ... (is) a series of transformations ultimately leading the church ... into the fullness of the kingdom ..." —not so much the transformation of a mystery already there, but the transformation of our perceptions "So that they may be to those that receive them ..." Christ transfigured (from the liturgy of St. John Chrysostom).

It is a quirk of the occidental mind to want things not only to be precise and punctual, but also to be systematically "thinkable" before we accept them. If so, now in the West, with all kinds of interrelational, transtemporal ideas floating around (existentialism, the "I–thou" of the Buber sort, process thinking, Gestalt systems in psychology, black and white holes in astronomy, field theory and interfield quarks in nuclear and astrophysics, science fiction, radio interreactions, E.S.P.), the idea of a wholly interconnecting faith community—one that is eschatological—becomes more thinkable. From their spirituality, Orthodox fellow Christians may be able to help westerners learn from such analogies to think metaphysically and to maintain the distinctions between that kind of clock time *(chronos)* and eschatology *(kairos)* as "thinkable"—the mystery of the church, the unending cosmic family reunion.

I hope so.

[2]The late Fr. Alexander Schmemann, Dean of St. Vladimir's Orthodox Theological Seminary in Crestwood, New York.

Scripture? Or Tradition?

"Professor, would you be kind enough to do the Scriptures for us this morning?"

The request was for early morning prayers at St. Paul's chapel of the International Center of the Orthodox Ecumenical Patriarchate near Geneva, Switzerland. I was guest of the center while doing some research on Orthodox-Lutheran relations, and attended Matins whenever possible. The priest in charge, Greek Orthodox, was a gracious host and friend, and I was honored to be asked.

Normally, Scriptures for the day were chanted rather than read. I thought of those basso-baritone deacons in cathedrals in Moscow and Sofia whose chanting boomed out like the voice of God bringing strength and encouragement to his people. My voice was a long way from that, even from Pavarotti's tenor. And normally at St. Paul's the chanting was in Greek or French. My Greek was barely adequate for traveling and Bible study, and my French needed polishing if sensitive French ears were not to be offended.

Father Paul sensed my reservations. "Just read it in English."

But what about those who understood little or no English? I remembered Father Schmemann's remark a few years ago. It was at a ten-day course for Orthodox and Lutheran clergy, jointly sponsored by Orthodox leaders and our Lutheran seminary in Chicago. "When it comes to reading Scripture you Lutherans seem to assume that you have to hear and understand every syllable in order to understand Scripture. There's a lot more to Scripture than that." That's the impression we had given with our meticulous, cerebral attention to "scientific" Bible study. Is there another, a holistic scriptural happening, the presencing of God and the biblical community, with whatever imperfections of pronunciation, whatever muffled syllables, whether chorused, or chanted, or read, in whatever languages?

I thought of those deeply moving Orthodox services I had shared in East Europe under Communist surveillance: wall-to-wall people, defiant, sometimes in tears, watchful icons, prayer candles, heady incense, *a capella* cantors and antiphonal choirs, prayers sung, Psalms and Scripture read and chanted, and Good News proclaimed. Not many, least of all I, could hear every syllable, or follow every statement. Yet all were caught up in a great movement of oneness, encouragement, renewal, hope, and peace.

Or again, I remembered meals with the students and faculty at the Orthodox seminary in Halki, Turkey. Here, the patriarch had gathered candidates for the priesthood from a score of countries around the world.[1] After grace was sung, I was ready for conversation with students around the table. Another surprise: from a podium at one end of the dining hall a student began to read from Holy Scriptures and continued throughout the meal, in Greek. For many new students from distant lands, and for me, it was a strange language, only dimly understood. But in a much deeper sense, it was a "conversing" across the centuries and across many geographic frontiers. "Scripture" was much more than

---

[1]The seminary was soon to be closed by an unsympathetic government. One hopes that it will be allowed to reopen by a later, more friendly government, not only for the sake of the Orthodox churches but as an enormous international benefit to the Turkish government.

concepts and instructions and ancient news reports that bade cerebral understanding. It was the extended biblical community in ongoing life and conversation together. And that puts a new spin on what Lutherans and Roman Catholics have been up to for the past 450 years in our debate about Scripture versus Tradition.

Tradition or Traditions?

Conventional wisdom among Lutherans has it that early Lutherans were Scripture-based, that Roman Catholics were tradition-based. The Protestant reformers were of course a varied lot, from radical iconoclasts who would dismantle all the "externals" of the established Roman church,[2] to moderates who desired to have some practices such as indulgences cleaned up, but who wished to remain within an ongoing Western catholic church. They were not dealing with Eastern Orthodoxy, which was hardly visible under Turkish occupation. Protestant reformers were dealing with Rome. In that struggle, to determine what was right and proper, they had to be concerned with objective norms, with authoritative tests: did authority derive from the pope? or councils? or Scripture? The argument came down finally to tradition or Scripture. What they saw as tradition in the Roman church they called human inventions, customs, "usages"; whereas Scripture was Holy Writ, Word of God, "divinely inspired." For Scripture to exercise its proper authority over the church, it would be necessary to leapfrog across Roman—human—traditions to get back to the divinely inspired written Word.[3] "Scripture alone" *(sola Scriptura)* became their rallying cry.

---

[2]Some radical reformers rejected—and some still reject—the use of creeds, sacraments, musical instruments, icons, statuary, altars, churchly buildings, and ordained ministry as either unscriptural or as interfering with the pure word of God. The "Zwickau prophets," a group of radical charismatics opposed to the Lutheran Reformation, even rejected the Scriptures, saying they didn't need Scriptures since "We have the Spirit."

[3]There were notable exceptions. Lutherans noted (*Augsburg Confession,* Article 26:40) that "many traditions are nevertheless kept among us—such as the order of lessons in the mass, holy days, etc. —which are profitable for maintaining good order in the church." And Melanchthon virtually equated Scripture and Tradition.

Luther, before his accusers at Wurms, declared: "Unless I am convicted (convinced) by Scripture and plain reason—I do not accept the authority of popes and councils, for they have contradicted each other—my conscience is captive to the Word of God." And the Lutherans' *Formula of Concord* declared from the start: "We believe, teach, and confess that the prophetic and apostolic writings of the Old and New Testaments are the only rule and norm according to which all doctrines and teachers alike must be appraised and judged …"[4] With that kind of history and concern about the necessity of objective norms for determining truth, church order, and personal conduct, it is perhaps not surprising that this struggle over authority would be at the start of nearly all of our contemporary Lutheran dialogues with Roman Catholics, Anglicans, and Orthodox.

So what and how is Scripture constituted? And what is Tradition? When and how do they function? For Orthodox churches, the question was not so much one of objective norm as of wholeness. Scripture is not so much objective authority *over* the church as it is participation of the apostolic biblical community *in* the church. How do they do that? During matins and vespers, the Psalms, all of them, are read each week; during Lent twice a week. Each year the entire New Testament is read during eucharistic services. The Divine Liturgy (regular worship), rich in colorful ethnic traditions and symbols, is also packed with biblical texts. Father Timothy Ware (now Bishop Kallistos) has pointed out that there are 98 Old Testament and 114 New Testament passages within the prayers, praise, and blessings of the liturgy. The Kyrie, hymns, prayers, exhortation, and blessings are couched in the language of Scripture.

Very near the beginning of the service, the priest and worship assistants do a procession, with candles and incense, from the altar, out among the people, and back to the gates before the altar. There the priest, who has carried the Holy Bible in the

[4]*The Book of Concord* (Fortress Press, Philadelphia, PA, 1959), p. 464.

procession, kisses the Bible and places it on the altar. This entire action—the procession, the "Holy God! Holy Mighty! Holy Immortal!" hymn, the prayers, the reading of the Epistle and Gospel, the homily—altogether the "Little Entrance," re-presents God's coming into the world, incarnate in Jesus Christ.[5] Scripture becomes alive; Word becomes flesh; Incarnation happens in the middle of the world. More than a "once upon a time," from procession and Scripture reading to homily among the people the Divine Liturgy is a recapitulation of God's perpetual coming forth into the world—the Holy Gospel. A continuing vestige of that among Lutherans is when the pastor, before the sermon, brings the Bible down the aisle of the nave and reads the Gospel lesson there in the midst of the congregation.

Is *that* Scripture reading merely a *reading* of Scripture? Is it Tradition? For Orthodox Christians, as for biblical scholars, that is too neat a distinction, historically and experientially. God's incarnation and self-revelation come to humankind first through seeing and hearing and telling, not writing and reading. Before there were written Scriptures, there were spoken reports, stories, sometimes legends of what Jesus did, what he said, where he went, what happened to him and around him—"oral tradition." We have no scriptures as such written by Jesus, and not everything about him was written in Scriptures. At the beginning was experience, of Jesus' person and of events—Christians telling and retelling their stories. Out of this great oral apostolic tradition some letters, reports, and stories were recorded and passed on *(Traditio)* as written tradition—that became a fixed core around which families of Christians gathered and carried on their conversation with past and future generations. But the presence of Christ and the inspiration of the Holy Spirit did not cease with the writing and gathering and approval (canonization) of specific texts by the early church. As an extension of and

---

[5]A later procession, the Great Entrance, is similar, but with the communion bread and wine, re-presenting the Holy Gifts of the Triune God for the world on the cross and in the Eucharist.

The Gospel is read in the midst of the congregation at Holy Communion Lutheran Church, Racine, Wisconsin. For both Orthodox (the "Little Entrance") and Lutherans, this signifies God's coming, incarnate in the world.

continuous with that, the community of believers formulated their worship, confessions of faith, prayers, theological writing, and way of life and governance with different accents in different places, languages, and cultures, all focussing around manifestations of God's presencing and the sharing, clarifying conversations in the living community of faith that such sharing evoked. It was a Living Tradition in which we, succeeding generations, were also to grow up and participate. Hence, it is not just the words of Scripture, printed black on white, that are there in the reading; the whole biblical community is there. Thus have Holy Scripture and Holy Tradition been inseparably bound together.[6] The

[6]In the 2nd century, C.E., Bishop Irenaeus of Lyon identified "the Holy Scriptures (as) the first written formulation of *Tradition*." Found in "Against Heresies," *Ante-Nicene Fathers, Vol. 1* (Christian Literature Publishing Co., Buffalo, NY, 1885).

point was driven home for me in teaching early church history: without the church as Living Tradition there would have been no Scripture. And without Scripture as a steady anchor, the church would not have survived.

Now, that gives Scripture a different kind of quality and consequently a different function than that of a book of rules. Indeed, even what are called the "Ten Commandments," in their origin, were not rules of behavior but identity affirmations from God. As Von Rad reminds us in his *Old Testament Theology*,[7] when the Israelites fled Egypt they saw themselves as nobodies: "We don't even have a god." To which God responded, "Yes, you do. You have a God. I, the one who brought you out of the land of Egypt, I am the Lord your God. And because you have a God you are a people, my people. And because you are a people who have a God, therefore you love your God and don't need graven images. Because you have a God you are a people who don't steal, who don't kill, who don't commit adultery ..." (Ex. 20:2). Only later, says Von Rad, did the scribes and clergy reduce these identity affirmations to rules of conduct. It was the affirmation from God that was primary and the basis for an ongoing living relationship. That ongoing affirmation, that continuous expression of presence, that Word become flesh, that Living Scripture, or as Lutherans might say that *viva vox evangelii* (living voice of the Gospel)—one doesn't just believe it or repeat it, one participates in it as believer, questioner, and proclaimer with the rest of the biblical community. Not just a book of rules or norms, but a whole world of connections, conversations, discussion, insight, mutual critique and encouragement.

Then, what is Tradition? For the Orthodox, Tradition is a living relationship in its fullness. It is Holy Tradition. Lossky[8] calls it "the life of the Holy Spirit in the Church." It

---

[7]Gerhard von Rad, *Old Testament Theology, Vol. 1* (Harper & Row, New York, 1962), Ch. B.

[8]Vladimir Lossky, *The Mystical Theology of the Eastern Church* (James Clarke & Co., Cambridge, England, 1973), p. 236 ff.

comprises, substantively, what is given in the Lord Jesus, preached by the apostles, preserved by the Fathers, and on which the church is founded. This means it is the living faith, its practice, substance, clarification, and transmission, that is, the life of the church in Christ and of Christ in the church. It both includes and is alongside the Living Scripture. And this Holy Tradition in its core and dynamic is one and undivided, unbroken—*Living* Tradition.

But there are also *traditions* in the church that are variations of historical, liturgical, linguistic, human, and cultural practices. These are changeable, are for the well-being of the church and world, but are nonetheless related to and conditioned by the Spirit in the church. Lutherans may note here the analogous distinction between Holy Tradition and traditions made by Lutherans and Saints Cyprian, Augustine, and others before them, between those things essential and those optional *(adiaphora)*. But they are all part of the living church's expression in this world, not to be jettisoned too readily, nor without good reason in light of the church's total calling.

In the past generation we, Lutherans and Orthodox, have had two rounds of dialogue in North America.[9] The first round focused on Scripture and Tradition. There is no official report from that round, but it is clear from the minutes and the papers read that much progress was made by our representatives, Lutheran and Orthodox, towards a shared understanding of (Living) Scripture and (Living) Tradition as mutually coinhering; that is, neither exists apart from the other. Each sustains, corrects, and illuminates the other: "Scripture and Tradition do not denote elements in the Christian faith which stand apart and in contrast to each other, but rather are inseparably related,"[10] reciprocally

---

[9]The first volume of the official report of the second round, J. Meyendorff and R. Tobias, eds., *Salvation in Christ, Vol. I* (see Introduction, note 7).

[10]Minutes of the first round of Lutheran-Orthodox Dialogue in North America, available from the author or the Department of Ecumenical Affairs, Evangelical Lutheran Church in America, Chicago, IL.

within each other. In Lutheran jargon it might be said, as of the Christic presence in the Eucharist, that each is "in, with, and under" the other: "in," as neither distant nor separate from the other; "with," as being distinguishable, not identical, but still one; and "under," as participating in the formation, each of the other.

The international Orthodox-Lutheran Joint Commission recognized this coinherence in its statement of 1985:[11]

> The Holy Scriptures are an inspired and authentic expression of God's revelation and of the experience of the Church *at its beginnings.* In the Church's ongoing experience of its life in Christ, in the faith, love and obedience of God's people and their worship, the Holy Scriptures become *a living book* of revelation which the Church's Kerygma, dogma and life may not contradict. Because through the guidance of the Holy Spirit the dogma of the Church is in agreement with the Holy Scriptures therefore the dogma itself becomes an unchangeable witness to the truth of revelation. Thus, under the guidance of the Holy Spirit, divine revelation is living in the Church through the Holy Scripture *and* Holy Tradition *(emphasis mine).*

In the living church, Scripture is alive, together with a very alive Tradition in all its fullness. If there is still an issue here between Lutherans and Orthodox it is at the fundamental level of ecclesiology: Is the church dependent upon a formal, objective authority for regulating its life, or is it a living eschatological community with a living faith in a living God and the provisional assurances and experiences of his presence along the way? That may well be a Lutheran problem.[12]

As a Lutheran sharing in large part that perception of, no, that participation in Living Tradition/Living Scripture, I was

---

[11]Available from the author or the Department of Ecumenical Affairs.

glad "to do the Scriptures" for us that morning, and many
other mornings.

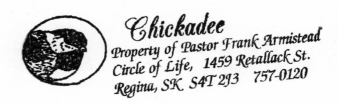

Chickadee
Property of Pastor Frank Armistead
Circle of Life, 1459 *Retallack St.*
Regina, SK S4T 2J3 757-0120

---

[12]Note to theologians: If Scripture is the crystallization of our perception of Divine
Self-presencing, in print, black on white, and if Tradition, which includes that, is the
lively *(via vitae)* practice of the communion in God that evokes, then one could do an
analogy of the relation of Scripture/Tradition/Church to the hypostatic union of the
Holy Trinity: in essence the same, i.e., consequences and carriers of Divine Self-
presencing, but each with its own "nature," a bearing of its own, not opposed, nor
contradictory, nor finished. For further data on Tradition and traditions, see the
report and working documents of the *Fourth World Conference on Faith and Order*, P. C.
Rodger and L. Vischer, eds. (Association Press, New York, 1964).

Love Me? Feed My Sheep

Most of the Orthodox families in North America have arrived in the last seventy-five years. They came from lands normally identified as East Europe and the Near East: Greece, Serbia, Russia, Rumania, Bulgaria, Turkey, Syria, and Lebanon. They have now grown to about 4.5 million members. During that same period, between 50 and 60 million Orthodox Christians died of other than natural causes in East Europe alone. In the golden days of Christendom in what is now Turkey, virtually the whole population of several million was Orthodox. Today, there are fewer than one thousand Orthodox Christians in Turkey. What happened?

For nearly 2,000 years Orthodox Christians have endured the onslaughts of all sorts of adversaries (Romans, Arians, Goths, Huns, Avars, Mongols, Tatars, Turks, Crusaders, Muslims, Nazis, Fascists, and Marxists), not to mention severe natural calamities such as earthquakes, floods, and famine, and not infrequently the efforts of fellow Christian proselytizers from the West. As to their faith, Stalin was right: It's "like a nail. The harder you hit it, the deeper it goes." Today one finds cathedrals in Moscow, Sofia, Bucharest, Belgrade, and Athens packed for the Divine Liturgy. On my last visits I found some 1,000 seminary students in Leningrad (St. Petersburg) and Zagorsk plus another 1,000 in extension programs preparing for the priesthood in Russia, more than 600 candidates in theological seminaries in Bucharest, and more than 2,000 theological students in Athens and Salonica. In Russia, despite very severe losses to Communist oppression, 65 percent of the population are Christian (almost identical to the percentage of Christians in North America), while in the republics of Georgia, Armenia, and the Baltics as many as 95 percent are estimated to be Christian. "… Afflicted in every way, but not crushed; perplexed, but not driven to despair; persecuted, but not forsaken; struck down, but not destroyed; always carrying in the body the death of Jesus, so that the life of Jesus may also be manifested in our bodies" (II Cor. 4:8–10). I am in awe of these people's faithfulness, their tenacity, and their ability to accept the blows of adversaries, hurt and wounded, and to come back with grace, courage, and the expectation of a better, win-win future for all.

Should we conclude that "adversaries" no longer threaten the Orthodox? Greek bishops wanted an explanation. "Who is it that is trying to make CARE parcel Methodists of Orthodox Christians? And why?" We were in the main lounge of a ship chartered by the Greek Orthodox Church, somewhere between Athens and Corinth. It was the 1900th anniversary of St. Paul's travels in Greece. The Greek Orthodox Church was hosting a special celebration, with ecumenical guests from many parts of the world, retracing St. Paul's route from Troas to Neapolis, Philippi, Salonica, Berea, Athens, Corinth, Nicopolis, and Rhodes. It was a grand occasion for us to get acquainted with our Orthodox hosts, young and old, to hear presentations on St. Paul and current ecumenical themes. For the Greeks it was a chance for refreshment after the privations of their long civil war. Villages and towns were still laid waste; there were serious shortages of food, medicines, clothing, shelter, utensils, and tools—everything. In the midst of that, zealous evangelicals from America were distributing CARE parcels to the needy, who were to sign a "receipt"—which turned out to be a membership registration for an American Methodist church!

G. Bromley Oxnam, Bishop of The Methodist Church in the United States, was on the hot seat, ringed by offended Greek bishops and lay leaders. "We want to know why you are proselytizing among our people—taking advantage of their hunger ..." "Don't we have a mutual commitment as fellow members of the World Council of Churches?" "We understand that to mean that we treat each other as sister churches. Why do you...?" Bishop Oxnam was squirming. He was embarrassed.

Sharing Ecumenical Commitment
As a Lutheran, I, too, have had some embarrassment over what appeared to be Lutheran proselytism. In 1555 a James Basilicus Marchetti appeared at the door of Luther's close colleague, Philip Melanchthon. Claiming descent from the kings of Epirus and from Heracles, and apparently aware that the Lutherans were interested in rapprochement with the Orthodox patriarchate of Constantinople, he convinced Melanchthon that he was a cousin of Patriarch Joasaph II, and that an alliance with the Orthodox could easily be arranged. Marchetti was in fact a slippery adventurer, probably the son of a Creton sailor, for twenty-two years in the army of Charles V. After leaving the Lutherans in Germany, he involved himself in military and political intrigues in Poland, then, with the help of Polish auxiliaries, overthrew Prince Alexander IV of Moldavia and assumed rule as King John I. Probably born Orthodox, likely sometime a Roman Catholic, now sympathetic to what he believed to be Lutheranism, John tried to "reform" the Moldavian Orthodox Church by closing monasteries, confiscating monastic properties, removing icons and relics from the churches, and appointing a Polish protestant as archbishop of Moldavia. In 1563 the Orthodox faithful rebelled, and John surrendered and was executed. In the meantime the Orthodox Ecumenical Patriarch in Constantinople had become so concerned as to ask the King of Poland to intervene against the "Lutherans." It's an embarrassment to nonproselytizing Lutherans even to this day.

There are several instances of sizable Lutheran presences in mainly Orthodox territories, not, however, resulting from proselytization. These communities are principally the result of planned immigrations of Germans *en bloc* sponsored by governmental leaders: by Peter the Great to St. Petersburg, by Catherine the Great to southern Russia and Ukraine, by King Stephen to Transylvania, and by Stalin to Siberia as World War II prisoners. But I'd like to believe that Lutherans, intentionally, do not proselytize. Indeed, one just about has to be born again—to Lutheran parents—to be accepted by Lutherans as a genuine Lutheran! There are, of course, exceptions. Orthodox churches have an official policy not to proselytize. With respect to other faiths, theirs is a "live and let live" policy. Nor do they even encourage members of other Christian churches to become Orthodox. Indeed, they have encouraged others who are theologically and spiritually inclined towards Orthodoxy to remain in their own churches:

> ... the Orthodox Church does not expect that other Christians be converted to Orthodoxy in its historical and cultural reality of the past and the present and to become members of the Orthodox Church. Its desire is that all should strive in their own churches and traditions to deepen the fullness of the apostolic faith embodied in a fully ecclesial life.[1]

However, when there are compelling reasons, non-Orthodox may be received into Orthodox churches, as in the cases of mixed marriages, or of theological and spiritual disaffection from an existing church membership.

Aboard ship, Bishop Oxnam tried to explain: "Those who you say are proselytizing are not part of my church ... " "How so? They are Methodists, and you are the American Methodists' presiding bishop." Bishop Oxnam tried again: "But they are Free Methodists, from Indiana. They do not

---

[1]*Orthodox Contributions to Nairobi* (World Council of Churches, Geneva, Switzerland, 1975), pp. 51–52.

belong to my church. I have no authority over them." It was a perfectly logical explanation—for an American accustomed to American religious pluralism. But in Greece, if you are Greek and Christian, you are Orthodox. If you are Orthodox you are Greek. There is a small Lutheran chapel in Athens. It is for diplomats and tourists from the north. The little Greek Evangelical Church is for some kind of quasi-Greeks with a long history of foreign connections and is accorded religious rights as a matter of religious freedom. But to try to take advantage of people's hunger, to proselytize from the historic faith, to start a divisive sect, with CARE parcels ...? The bishop's explanation was stated clearly enough, but hard to understand: Doesn't Methodist mean Methodist? Like the situation of pioneer Orthodox lay people newly arrived in North America, it was hard for them to distinguish between evangelistic Protestants who proselytize, and evangelical Lutherans who don't. But the deeper question behind exploitation of hunger and disaster needed attention: What does shared ecumenical commitment mean? What is the understanding of that commitment for a Western church leader? Is it different from a "people's church" under-standing? Absolute individual freedom of choice? What about corporate responsibility and consultation?

It was nearly a decade ago that the Anglican communion approved in principle the possibility of ordaining women to the priesthood. Shortly thereafter the Anglican archbishop paid an official visit to the Russian Orthodox patriarch in Moscow. According to my informant, the Anglican arch-bishop rather playfully teased the patriarch: Why don't you get up-to-date with the modern world like we have? The patriarch was—politely—furious. Not because the Anglicans had made their own decision about the ordination of women. That could be discussed. But these two churches, the Russian Orthodox and the Church of England, were well along in their dialogue and negotiations towards mutual recognition. It was like when a couple is engaged to be married, and one partner unilaterally decides to change their future plans about children, home, or love, without consulting the other partner. What does any degree of "in communion" mean about mutual consultation? That sort of thing has happened to the Orthodox before, e.g., when the Roman church decided unilaterally to alter the original Nicene Creed of the undivided church by adding "and the Son" to the way the Holy Spirit proceeds. The theological issues involved in that could have been, and recently have been seriously discussed. (As a consequence Lutherans have agreed to the use of the unaltered original.) But the process of making unilateral decisions without consultation reflects a serious flaw in ecclesial understanding, which is unacceptable between churches desiring to reach or to maintain unity. Lutherans will need to remember that with respect to our own consecration of women as bishops. Consult first, in the context of dialogue and negotiation, not *ex post facto*—if we value our Orthodox relationships and dialogue.

Ground Rules for Mutual Respect

At various times in the past, ecumenical initiatives have noted some elementary principles of respect and responsibilities with regard to proselytism, jurisdiction, mutual support, and correction. That could and should be done again, updated, on a broad basis to include all World Council member churches and the Vatican—especially the Vatican and independent evangelicals—in light of recent entanglements and future developments in East Europe. Let me illustrate.

It was 1946. World War II was over. As an unwilling ally of Nazi Germany, Rumania was technically under the governance of the Allied Control Commission. A peace treaty was under consideration at Paris, but clouds on the eastern horizon looked anything but peaceful. A twenty-six-passenger DC-3 had brought the Rumanian delegation to Paris to negotiate terms of the peace treaty. The plane, loaded with used tires stacked to the ceiling, started the return flight with me as the sole passenger at the very rear of the plane.

Over the Alps the storm hit. The plane was tossed like a leaf in the wind, and tires flew everywhere. When we came out of the clouds above Austria, crew members worked their way to the rear through the jumble of tires. "Are you still here?" In the following days in Rumania and Bulgaria I sometimes wondered whether I would be.

Rumanian hospitality was at its very best, despite war-time shortages for the populace. I had just been elected officer of the postwar World Federation of Democratic Youth (only later to discover how dominated it was by Marxists) and that gave me *carte blanche* to travel Soviet-occupied East Europe. I was also on the staff of the World Council of Churches, and we needed to know what was happening to churches as the Soviet army liberated East European countries from Nazi and Fascist occupation. Rumanian Prime Minister Petru Groza and President Anna Pauker received me cordially and shared some of their vision of what a new democratic Rumania would be like. A few young Soviet soldiers were on the streets and in the cafes, quite willing to discuss the kind of homesickness, disillusionment, and hopes for a better world characteristic of young soldiers just about anywhere. The young King Michael, who was under virtual house arrest in his modest summer palace in the mountains, filled me in over lunch about the last days of Nazi occupation. On the very last day, as Soviet troops approached Rumania, he had gathered and led the students and other patriots in Bucharest in a bold uprising that defeated and forced the Nazi troops and Iron Guard to flee. Soviet troops then moved in and took credit for the liberation of Rumania. Shortly thereafter Vishinsky arrived from Moscow, expecting to have King Michael's signature on a document of surrender and abdication. The king refused. Vishinsky was furious. As he stormed out of the king's dining room, he threw the glass inkwell down on the table so hard that it cut a deep imprint in the table top. Angrily stomping out, he slammed the door so hard that the door posts were pulled out of the wall. Another Vishinsky legacy that we discovered later was a secret

"Vishinsky Plan" for the domestication of churches in Soviet-occupied East Europe.[2] One critical measure in that plan was to cut off relations between indigenous churches and religious bodies in the West. To understand one of the reasons and results of that, we need to step back in history.

In 1698 Transylvania (now part of Rumania) was annexed to the Austrian Empire, which was predominantly Roman Catholic, with a strong minority of Calvinists. Orthodox believers in the area, harassed by Calvinists and tempted by Jesuit promises, were pressured by the government to unite with Rome. Finally, the Metropolitan of Alba-Julia summoned 1,617 Orthodox clergy, most of whom reluctantly agreed to yield to Jesuit offers and government threats and to sign an act of submission to the Vatican as a "Uniate" church. It was not the people's choice. The priests who refused were defrocked. All were cut off from mother and sister Orthodox churches in Rumania by the newly established border. However, former Orthodox parishes, now called "Uniate," were allowed to keep their Orthodox liturgy and parish practices (hence, later to be called "Eastern Rite Catholics").[3]

In 1948, on the 250th anniversary of that forced act of submission, the "Uniate" Orthodox churches of Transylvania were reunited with the Orthodox Church of Rumania, again by governmental intervention. Some of the measures used by the Rumanian government to achieve that were highly questionable, some violent. Actually, the Rumanian government led by Petru Groza (who had told me in 1946 that he was the son of an Orthodox priest and himself a professing Orthodox), cared little for either the Orthodox or Uniates—or

---

[2]See my *Communist-Christian Encounter in East Europe* (School of Religion Press, Indianapolis, IN, 1956), p. 321.

[3]Some more recent "converts" were not so fortunate. During World War II, when Serbian Orthodox faithful in Croatia were threatened by the Catholic Ustashe (collaborators with Nazis and Fascists), "convert or die," 750,000 Orthodox including women, aged, and children were massacred, many in their own churches after submitting to forced "conversion." Catholic Archbishop Stepinac was tried and sentenced for complicity in carrying out the massacres.

for any religion for that matter. However, to prevent Western "subversive activities" they wanted to sever Uniate ties to the very powerful Western Vatican "empire." And that was to be achieved by reestablishing the pre-Uniate churchly jurisdictions that prevailed from roughly 1000 to 1700 C.E.

For us now, it is important to remember that the return of former Orthodox to Orthodoxy is a correction of a wrong forced on them centuries before, not a subversive act of proselytism by contemporary Orthodox churches. Further, what happened in Rumania in 1698, forced "conversion" of Orthodox to Roman Uniatism, also happened in Galicia, Ukraine, Czechoslovakia, and other Russian border areas. A similar attempt was made in Bulgaria, with limited success. As in Rumania, Communist governments after World War II took steps to reintegrate these Uniate Orthodox into the canonical Orthodox churches.

Now that the Soviet structures and Marxist control have disintegrated, certain agencies of the Vatican have revived their programs of uniatism and proselytism in what they regard as once again a "promising mission field" and are seeking such support as can be gained from Western powers.[4] Further, with the Russian Orthodox Church very seriously depleted in resources and trained leadership, eager peddlers bringing relief goods, Bibles, and tempting promises with strings attached are poised to do their proselytic business.[5] It is not a pretty picture, and bears our earnest prayers, as clear a view of history as possible, as much ecumenical statesmanship as can be mustered, and full disclosure in the courts of ecumenical and world opinion as to what exactly is happening. A Joint International Commission for Theological Dialogue between the Roman Catholic Church and the Orthodox churches has spelled out some ground rules for

[4]See "U.S. Bishops' Statement" in *Origins* (National Catholic News Service, Washington, DC, Dec. 8, 1988).

[5]"Uniatism," *Ecumenical Trends* (Graymoor Ecumenical and Interreligious Institute, Garrison, NY, Dec. 1993).

A good shepherd feeding his sheep

mutual respect in the face of historic tensions, economic imbalances, and proselytizing. That has yet to be accepted and implemented by the Vatican. Some kind of similar ground rules are overdue among evangelical Protestant churches, especially in view of their current race into East Europe to make "Christians" of Eastern Orthodox Christians.[6] The problem is further complicated when conservative evangelicals claim as a primary concern the individual "convert's" absolute "freedom of choice" over against corporate responsibility and decision-sharing. In any case, as we saw in Greece, one's freedom of choice is not too wide an

_____

[6]A recent publication of the Wycliffe Bible Translators (*In Other Words,* July-August, 1993, p. 4), who ought to be well enough informed to know better, refers to Russia as "the country hidden for years behind the Iron Curtain, closed to the gospel of Jesus Christ." Wycliffe Translators appears to be unaware that the Russian Orthodox Church lost more than 45,000 priests, nearly 1,000 monasteries, 60 seminaries, and 62,000 churches and chapels under Communist oppression, and still numbers 65 percent of the Russian population, almost exactly the same percentage as baptized Christians in the U.S.

option if one's children are cold and starving and someone offers food, clothing, funds, and hope, with or without attached strings.

In the world of relations between nations we have a United Nations to establish specific terms for "cease-fire," and peace observer teams to ensure compliance. Between *de facto* competing religious groups, do we need a "united churches truce commission" and observer teams to ensure compliance, perhaps even to facilitate supporting one another? It may come to that.

As a concluding model, I cite the story of a man whom I knew as Dean of the Faculty of Theology at the University of Salonica. He was born to Greek parents and baptized Orthodox. While still a baby his parents were killed in the Greek civil war. He was adopted by the pastor of the international chapel in Salonica and his wife. Though themselves German and Lutheran, they raised him as fully Greek, in the Orthodox faith, and with mother-tongue competences in English, German, and Greek languages. When I met him he was a respected theological professor, a gracious ecumenical host, and international diplomat for the Greek Orthodox Church.

"If you love me," it is possible to "feed my sheep," without trying to steal them.

Winter and Spring

Living in a culture preoccupied with death—whether to prevent it, or to defy it, or to cause it—I think I'm learning something from others living in the midst of it, or perhaps beyond it.

I didn't know for sure why Patriarch Gavrilo wanted me to visit Vrsac. It was a desolate corner of Yugoslavia, bordered by Rumania on the north and Bulgaria on the east. It was exactly the route the Soviet Union and its Comintern satellites would take if they decided to punish this upstart Communist Yugoslavia for declaring its independence from the Kremlin and the Comintern. Along that route, farms, which had been shelled and bombed in the war against the Axis (Nazi/Fascist) forces, were mostly abandoned. It was a no-man's land, where men risked being shot on sight. And I was on my way there to visit a ruined monastery.

Like many others, but with less reason, by 1950 I was weary of devastation and the wintry pall of death: central Warsaw a desert of churned bricks and charred rubble, Lidice and Oradour and numerous other towns obliterated for harboring anti-Nazis, earthquakes in the Dodecanese Islands, fifteen Protestant pastors in Bulgaria on trial as "American spies," the hopes of Rumanians shattered with the exile of their king, guerrilla war in all but the larger cities of Greece, and

Salonica, though badly damaged and suffering a very severe winter, still a haven for families fleeing guerrilla warfare. I had just been there, in midwinter, visiting refugees in an abandoned factory: windows out, cold winter rain through holes in the roof, muddy concrete floors; families from the guerrilla war huddling around open fires on the floor, cooking watery soup, trying to keep warm with ragged clothing and few blankets; air thick with smoke and the smell of dirt and animals; rats and fleas everywhere. Behind a cardboard partition a young woman was trying to comfort newly-born twins: cold, hungry, wrapped in rags, lying on reed mats on the floor. She lifted one baby towards me, pleading: "Take one. I cannot feed them and there is no milk." We, American Lutheran, Orthodox, and Protestant churches, did pour eighty million dollars' worth of foods, medicines, clothing, and blankets into those needs in the first eight months of that year, and it helped—though it was still not enough. And now, another visit to another place of need, a crippled monastery.

As early as the 14th century, the Serbian Orthodox Church had at least 2,000 monasteries scattered through the hills, mountain passes, river valleys, and sites of historic events. For five centuries under Muslim Turk occupation, that was where history, culture, and civilization were preserved, education promoted, farmers and villagers defended, and the faith of Christians anchored. During the war, many monasteries became fortifications, in turn, for neighboring farmers and shepherds, for Yugoslav loyalists, for Partisans, Nazis, Ustashis, and downed Allied fliers. None came through unscathed. Some have since been repaired to serve as orphanages, or for health programs or training centers. Many will probably never be restored. Others still serve as symbols of all that is good, hopeful, beautiful, and eternal in human existence. Near Vrsac, as villagers returned from the twilight and rubble of war to begin again, many hoped to find their monastery there as a refuge and beacon of new hope and a new future.

Through the Devastation

As we approached the monastery, jagged remains of walls became visible through the shell-splintered fruit trees. We stepped through or over ruined walls into the monastery gardens—there were no monks, but three Orthodox nuns in black habits greeted us. Not the least embarrassed that their habits were soiled and frayed from chipping stone, mixing mortar, digging soil, and planting crops, they could not have been more hospitable. We should have rolled up our sleeves to lend a hand! But, no, it was nearly lunch time and this was their place. Mother Helena, fluent in a half-dozen languages, as elegant, gracious, aristocratic as anyone I've known, welcomed us with all the warmth characteristic of Orthodox hosts in that part of the world, and more. Hers was an inspiring story.

Before and during World War II Helena and her husband had been ambassadors to Paris for the royal Yugoslav government. By the end of the war their government had been ousted, and nothing but prison awaited them as royalists if they returned to Communist Yugoslavia. All was lost. Helena and her husband made a suicide pact. He succeeded. She did not. Then came the anguishing process of grief, remorse, forgiveness, and new life. If all was lost, so were the insecurities that go with creaturely abundance. She was now liberated. There was nothing more to lose; everything to be gained. She committed herself to her church's ministry in whatever desolate situation might need her. That meant returning to Yugoslavia. The patriarch recommended Vrsac. And here she was, with two other nuns, in a border area unsafe for men, restoring a shattered and abandoned monastery and its chapel, gardens, and farm. When the neighboring farmers and their families returned, here would be the beacon and refuge they hoped for, as well as a spiritual leader and counselor. Here they would restore no-man's land to God's land, resurrected to new life from destruction and virtual death.

Years later, I was teaching at a seminary in America. One noon, another professor and I took two of our students from South Africa to lunch off-campus. It was winter. The sycamores and oaks were, of course, bare. As we alighted from the car, one student remarked to the other: "Isn't it sad? They are so dead." As South Africans they had never known the bleakness of winter. How could they know in their bones the fantastic newness of life called "spring"? Dramatist Arthur Miller, after family, friends, wife, Party, and co-workers, abandoned him, was devastated, suicidal. But then, having "hit bottom," and experiencing some kind of personal resurrection, he was able to affirm boldly that thereafter "I wake up every morning a new boy."[1]

Winter vs. spring? Death vs. life? Have we probed and appropriated the spiritual meanings of that connection? Saint Anthony (4th century, C.E.) fled to the desert, lived in the tombs to challenge the claims of Death and the presumption that death was the antithesis of life. Again and again the psalmist cries "out of the depths unto thee" (Psalm 130:1). Surely there is truth in that; that it is out of the depths, out of winter, out of tragedy, out of hell that we perceive and appropriate spring and blessing and life and heaven. But are they really totally opposed to each other?

I sensed that for Mother Helena and others of her faith it was more than opposition. I have often wished to go back and continue that conversation. For her and her Sisters, I think it was not a matter of devastation *or* restoration, of death *or* life. It was both. Death is not the denial, the final denial, of life. In life, in spring, in joy, there is already the dying of what was. And in dying, in winter, in tragedy there is already new life. Death is not the final enemy of life, but a transitional passageway of larger life. Resurrection, yes, it involves death, real death, but it's not death-without-life. As surely as Mother Helena and the Sisters knew that the seeds they planted would die and rise again, in fact, were never *not* alive, so they

---

[1] Arthur Miller, *After the Fall* (Viking Press, New York, 1964).

After the devastation of World War II, young people in
Bulgaria build a railroad through a mountain pass,
mostly with hand tools.

knew in their faith that resurrection is already part of life
along with dying. Yes, they walked "through the valley of the
shadow of death," through death, not just the foretaste of it,
which eschatologically also had its brooks and springs of life.
The farmers' homes and fields around them were not to be
merely restored. In their continuum, as in Plato's *idee*, planted
there by God, in their continuum from before, through,
and after devastation, their homes, fields and new life were
resurrected, never totally nullified *(nihil)*. For us in the
Christian faith, every Sunday is both crucifixion and resurrection day.

 As we finished the delightful lunch that Mother Helena and
her Sisters had prepared for us from their garden, the birds
overhead and on the broken walls seemed to echo that certi-
tude. After a brief prayer in the chapel-under-reconstruction,
we said our goodbyes and shared a final: "Pray for us." I was

renewed and ready for another visit to another place of
devastation—and resurrection.

If it was the patriarch's intention for me to go to Vrsac to
encourage and provide assistance to Mother Helena, he had
it backward. He couldn't know that no one would be more
richly blessed by that visit than I (or did he?). Similarly, who
could have known, out of the Nazi and Soviet and Turkish
devastation that Orthodox fellow Christians from east and
southeast Europe had gone through—intellectuals, musi-
cians, poets, authors, composers, priests, theologians,
workers, all "refugees"—who could have known what an
incredibly rich blessing they would bring to Western
churches and society?

American Culture and Our Commonalities

There are today in North America about 5,300,000 members[1] of the canonical Orthodox churches; 8,625,000 Lutherans. Ancestors of the Orthodox were mostly Greeks, Russians, Serbians, Rumanians, Bulgarians, Albanians, and Syrians. Ancestors of the Lutherans were mostly Germans and Scandinavians, with more recent additions of Africans, Asians, and Hispanics. Scandinavian ancestors of Lutheran immigrants had established colonies on the eastern seaboard nearly 500 years before America's "discovery" by Columbus, but these colonies had disappeared by the time our Lutheran forebears began arriving, some 40,000 in the late 1600s, 4,000,000 in the mid-1880s. Orthodox missionaries from Russia arrived in Alaska as early as 1794, and a small colony of Greek sponge fishers was established in the 1700s in Florida, but the main tide of Orthodox immigrants arrived in the first half of the 20th century.

Nearly all of our ancestors, Orthodox and Lutheran, arriving in America were lay people. What they found here was a strange and wonderful place. The predominant language, English, was different. The predominant religion, Calvinist and Unitarian, was different. The structures of government, no kings or princes, separation of church and state, were different. The churches were different: nonhierarchical,

[1]When affiliated living relatives are included.

67

"gathered" individual believers, many evangelists and lay preachers, virtually no priests, pastors, or bishops. (Even Lutherans didn't get around to having bishops until 1988.) On that kind of frontier and in that unfamiliar culture, Lutherans and Orthodox have found that they have a very great deal in common with one another.

Communality

Americans take pride in their "rugged individualism." They declare their own taxes. They throw their own tea parties! They resist regimentation. They choose their own diets and dress. They carry their own rifles. They drive their own cars. They build their own detached private houses. They are inclined to trespass when it suits them. They choose their own vocations and their colleges and training programs. They choose their own friends, and doctors, and preachers, and churches, and they decide their own beliefs according to their own tastes. They choose their own spouses, and they may choose to drop the first one for another, and another, and another. The options available for unhindered choices, whether in breakfast cereals, or banks, or political parties, or religions, or spouses, or cars, or stocks, or communications systems, provide a perplexing playground and are a psychiatrist's delight, for we have foresworn the ancient securities of group/family decision, and have generally not yet mastered the sophisticated evaluative processes necessary for sound individual decision-taking. We enjoy the freedom of it all, but, ah, the wreckage and responsibility! That is one side of the American ethos. But it's not the only one.

In a culture that champions individualistic "rights," Orthodox and Lutherans in America are distinguishable by their sense of communality, of corporate, familial (sometimes clannish) responsibility and common destiny. We were nurtured communally. Our mother churches were communal, not just voluntary gatherings of individually saved believers who elected on their own to join. Lutheran churches were called *volkskirchen,* the people's churchly community. Greeks under Turkish occupation were *rummillet,* a self-governing, self-continuing community within the Turkish culture. In Russia, the churches again are *sobornal*—they do what they do as a whole, familially, in council, not as the sum of individualistic parts. Each believer, each congregation participates in all, past, present, and future. When a candidate is to be ordained, church leaders nominate the candidate, but unless the whole people together respond with their confirming *"axios"* (he is worthy), there is no ordination. In the Lutheran tradition, the combined voice of synod, seminary, and bishop may nominate a candidate for ordination, but until a congregation of believers sees fit to "call" the candidate, the candidate is not ordained. And when ordained, it is not just a private act bestowed on the individual ordinand, nor yet only by the local congregation: the ordinand is ordained within, by, and for the whole church. There are also close parallels of total communal involvement in marriage and baptism. That is one reason why those rites normally take place in the eucharistic service.

The roots of our communality reach far back in history. For example, Russian Orthodox *soborny* is traced at least as far back as the ancient clan or village, the *obschina,* where decision-taking began when the elders or chiefs came to what they regarded as the wisest course of action on a given matter. Their proposal was then put to the whole commune, which would decide "yes" or "no" or "back to the drawing board" for further consideration and a new proposal. It was a total communal process, decision by consensus, as in the Native Americans' tribal council. In that kind of familial process, the politics of decision-taking did not need several "parties" locked in adversarial combat (win-lose) until one party won by a 51 percent majority. Slow, perhaps; the process was extended until all concerns were dealt with and a consensus reached. And with those kinds of roots, one can understand more readily how the one-party Marxist system could hold sway in the former Soviet Union as long as it did. One "party" had been enough when it truly incorporated everyone and everyone's concerns.

But what if an aristocratic elite with the necessary power takes control, heedless of the masses, imposing an either-or, win-lose solution between elitist directives and vulnerable masses, as in the former Soviet Union, or Roman Christendom, or America before the War of Independence? First of all, that is a disruption of the spiritual base of oneness that makes communality and shared decision-taking possible. If it comes to that—whether by intention or default of the elite or the masses—then better to go with the "natural language" of the masses, says nuclear physicist Werner Heisenberg in his *Physics and Philosophy,* where the highest aspirations of striving creatures and the ground out of which they come most nearly coincide, rather than with the abstract conceptualizations of closeted "experts." That is fundamentally what happened with the Reformation and with American independence. The "very ground was crying out" through the masses—*kata holos,* according to the whole—truly "catholic."

Properly exercised, our communality enjoys a complementarity of functions: a healthy dynamic of individual responsibility and expression on the one hand, and communal care and decision on the other. That is indeed operative in our Lutheran and Orthodox behavior in America, though in this privatistic culture it is often our communality (clannishness?) that is most apparent to outsiders. In our dialogue partnership we approach each other as churches, as communities, not merely as individuals sharing private opinions. Such communality, carried to extreme, to exclusive tribalism, can be a weakness; but the answer to that is not radical individualism, rather a more thoroughgoing communality.

Complementarity of Separated Church and State
How does a new nation regulate the relations between church and state? Should the state direct and control all activ-

The author (left) talks with Rumanian Prime Minister Petru Groza about Rumanian hopes and church-state relations, shortly after liberation from the Nazis and before control by the Soviets. The prime minister wanted to assure me (and the West) that church-state relations would continue on a mutually supportive basis. After all, he was an Orthodox Christian, his father an Orthodox priest. Michael was still on the throne as God's monarch over both church and state— Byzantine *symphonia* style—and nearly 90 percent of the people were members of both church and state. Soon thereafter new leadership under Soviet control took over the government, the king was deposed and exiled, and the church was subjected to Soviet controls outlined in the Vishinsky Plan. Recently, with the downfall of the Communist regime, a new era of complementarity between church and state seems to be under way.

ities within its borders including religion and education? Or, should the church, as ordained of God, direct the activities of all in its domain, including the state, to the end that the City of God (per St. Augustine or John Calvin) and kingdom of heaven might be realized? Or, should there be a complementary, collaborative "division of labor," as in Sweden or Greece?

By the time Lutheran and Orthodox immigrants became involved in that issue, other European immigrants had already decided it: there would be separation of church and state. That didn't mean Lutherans and Orthodox did not have ideas and a contribution to make. Through centuries of testing and being tested, from Constantine through Turkish occupations, the Orthodox had arrived at a principle of *symphonia* between church and state. The church has its responsible functions under God, and the state has its sphere of responsibility, also under God. Ideally, they work as a complementary team.[2] Lutherans from north Europe and Scandinavia also had their *symphonia;* they called it "two realms." One is the realm of the state, of secular responsibility; the other is the realm of the church. Both are ordained of God to their proper responsibilities, and should complement one another. So they interpreted it in America. Church and state are separated but not adversarial. They should be complementary. Unlike some other American religious groups that would have had the church (*their* church) controlling the secular government (theocracy), or others that would have been quite prepared to have the church be an instrument directed and supported by the state, and still others that would, and did, flee from secular government involvements into isolated religious communes, not so Orthodox and Lutherans. Both intended complementarity of purpose, function, and ideology between church and state that would require disciplined encounter and cautious cooperation. In that complementarity believers are encouraged to exercise their full responsibilities as both citizens of the state and members of the Body of Christ.[3]

[2]As historical manifestation of that complementarity, the emperor was head of both church and state and representative of God over both, with a prime minister to run the affairs of state and a patriarch to direct the life of the church. Real or symbolic vestiges of such arrangements can be found in several present monarchies and in some cathedrals of former monarchies, where the principal "throne" in the cathedral is designated for God's emperor, and another lesser throne for the head of the church.

[3]While some power-hungry secular authorities and clerics disregard the bounds of *symphonia* and "two realms," that does not invalidate intended complementarity *per se.*

Goals? Or Doxological Ethics?

What is really right? Or not right? How is that determined in America? Whatever we may say about biblical commandments, in popular culture-religion in America, value and morality are determined by what works, that is, according to what benefits or advances the welfare of the controlling "majority," whether in economics, education, ecology, esthetics, law, sports, or social custom. Management by Objective (MBO) adds to that, saying that net benefits should be measurable, soon. If social status, business advantage, and good citizenship are enhanced by attendance at the right churches: encourage right church attendance. If financial growth and stability, mutual trust, and electability are strengthened by honesty at the bank and in the marketplace: be honest. If prospects of liberation for the oppressed are improved when supported by a well-reasoned ideology: do liberation theology. "Enlightened self-interest" and "Protestant work ethic" describe the driving force of our cultural ethic; the "objective," the desired end, becomes master. We design our means to achieve prescribed ends and call it success! Populist triumphalism.

It would be wrong to suggest that Lutherans and Orthodox are not involved in that process, or that everyone else is. It is nonetheless true that Lutherans and Orthodox in principle work out their axiology, their ethics, in the context of doxology, of responsive praise and thanksgiving to God for what God has already done, not just to predispose what he might do. And that allows a certain distance, even liberation, from over-concern with immediate benefits. That which is response towards God, with and in God, may eventually bring blessing to our earthly existence. But that is not guaranteed, not immediately. It may bring martyrdom. Nonetheless, one asks first, not "Does a proposed course of action secure expected benefits?" but "Is it true to what God has done?" Thus a Lutheran Bonhoeffer can stand up to Hitler and Orthodox Ecumenical Patriarch Gregory V can stand up to

Turkish conquerors, and be martyrs. Their martyrdom is an everlasting statement concerning true value—and its Source.

In the American scene, where bloody martyrdom at the hands of the state is unlikely for most of us, where Orthodox and Lutherans presuppose complementarity between church and state, we hold that it is the rightful responsibility of the state on behalf of all the people to administer the marketplace, and it is the business of the church to speak, sometimes to thunder prophetically, to the state about the way and the reasons for doing that. For this cause (*martyria* as witness to the grace and glory of God), Orthodox Archbishop Iakovos—as did his predecessors—developed a pattern of periodic meetings to offer special insight to our national presidents, often at their request, and our Lutheran churches have created advocacy offices in Washington, New York (the United Nations), and state capitols—in doxology to God and hopefully a benediction to our nation.

Christology and Soteriology

Much of mainline Protestantism in America has become almost unrecognizably deformed. Evidences of that[4] when traced to their common source reveal a Christology that is operationally adoptionist.[5] "Adoptionist," that is, that God called or sent this nice young man from Nazareth to do his job on earth while God is off somewhere else doing his main business. Jesus is seen by these Protestants (in company with Unitarians, Jews, and Muslims) as a great prophet, teacher, noble example, and martyr, but not quite himself God.

There are at least three reasons for the prevalence of this heresy among us. One comes from serious respect for the Almightiness, the wholly Otherness, the Transcendence of

---

[4]Eclectic, syncretistic ecumenical and interfaith liturgies, some proposals for church unions, the so-called "Jesus Seminar," certain documents of the Consultation on Church Union (COCU) and the National Council of Churches, which apparently assume that deeply held positions of faith and tradition are ultimately "negotiable."

[5]Or Arian or Ebionite.

God. If God is all that "high and lifted up," pure, undefiled, perfect, then if he wants something done amid our grubbiness, he does it via lesser lieutenants. How could we respect a smudged God? The second reason is that we want to be saved. And therefore we see Jesus for what he *does* for us— our guide, example, sacrifice, ransom, saver—more than what Jesus *is* in himself. Not so much Emmanuel—God with us—as an agent sent to do something *to* us and *for* us. And so Christology becomes soteriology. The third reason is sloppy language. Even in the most correct theological circles we frequently slip into the use of the word "God" as though only God the Father were God (hymns and abbreviated liturgies are full of it). Granted, as human beings we cannot fathom the internal mysteries of the Holy Trinity, but we do know enough to perceive that in the immanent tri-unity, the essence of God, there are three Persons: God the Father, God the Son, and God the Holy Spirit, hypostatically three in one and one in three. There never was a time when all were not. Each is God. All are God.

The critical operational problem about the adoptionist heresy is that "good news" is not so much a message about what God is like as it is about the means, methods, rites, or whatever it takes to "save" us. And that preoccupation blurs our seeing that what is really *good* news is that there is something about God that makes God want to be with us. From God's perspective, it might be that God became human to do something to us or for us. But from our perspective, it is more a matter of God being God—what his incarnation says to us about the nature of God—that is of prior import. Serious attention is needed here to clean up any confessional or liturgical or hymnic language that identifies as means those events that are first of all consequences celebrative of God-being-here, including sacraments, before they are instruments to get-God-here or to get-us-there.

In these matters and in this culture, it is clear that Lutherans and Orthodox stand solidly together with the Fathers of

Nicaea-Constantinople: Christ is "eternally begotten of the Father, God from God, Light from Light, true God from true God, begotten, not made, of one Being with the Father." *Therefore* we know the love and presence of the Father.

A Special Priesthood

"In this country anyone can be a minister. God ordains whom he pleases." That is a popular presupposition in American religious history. Whether springing from radical individualism or from distrust of bishops and ecclesiastical despotism, it has proliferated into thousands of unrelated religious groups, each attached to its particular guru, holding its own peculiar tenets. Such pluralism ranges in leadership from the spontaneous "Spirit urged" to speak in itinerant evangelists' revivals or charismatics' meetings, to the carefully crafted leadership of a mega-congregation of 20,000 members, or of radio/TV "churches" at a distance from millions of adherent-contributors.

Lutherans and Orthodox affirm that God does indeed call, equip, and ordain persons for special priestly ministries, whose primary obedience and accountability are to God. But that is exercised within and not apart from the community of God's people. That includes the lay people, without whose affirming responsibility (whether congregational "call" or congregational *axios*—"he is worthy") there is no ordination. It also includes the representation of the whole church universal through the bishops, without whose blessing there is again no ordination. So, the special priesthood is in principle by and to the whole church through appropriate spiritual and organizational processes. There are in principle no "lone ranger" priests/pastors in our two churches.

There has, however, been some evolution in this country in the way lay members and bishops are involved. As was pointed out by an Orthodox participant in the first round of Lutheran-Orthodox dialogues, in America there has been a tendency for Orthodox parishes to become increasingly "congregational," and for Lutherans to become increasingly "hierarchical." Understandably so. As Orthodox laity have become more articulate in America they have balanced the voice of the clergy with that of the laity. While Lutherans, lacking bishops on the American frontier and therefore having been more congregational, now recognize the ecclesial reality and historical need for closer networking and interdependence through an appropriate episcopacy. In both cases, a more holistic participation in mutual ministry is the result. Perhaps our paths already converge just over the horizon, or will when we have dealt with the question of "specialness" of ordination in relation to sacramentality.

Specialness? Our clergy (some Lutherans and most Orthodox) even wear distinctive street garb, which has again brought encouragement and blessing along the byways and ghettos. Not so in East Europe. There it was against the law. In Communist Rumania it didn't matter that much. In Marxist Bulgaria, some overly appreciative and a few hostile glances on the street convinced me that my clerical garb wasn't publicly acceptable. In newly secularized Ataturk Turkey, Orthodox friends forewarned me of new laws proscribing distinctive religious garb. And in the former Soviet Union, a long history of suppression and massacre of the clergy made clear that if we clergy went on the street, it must be in street clothes. Whatever the perception and intention of the rulers of those countries (the most charitable, that they wished to "level the playing field" for all citizens), I was prompted to reflect on my own perception and intention about the meaning of ordained clergy in the marketplace. Was our specialness and our distinctive dress a matter of liturgical, sacramental function, and was preaching, comforting, teaching, and administrative leadership a matter of functional effectiveness, whether we were selected from within the people of God or dispatched from without to the people of God? Or was it a quality of being, provided by God, out of which has followed a wide variety of functions?

When Orthodox and Lutheran laity come together with their priests and pastors, their awareness of something very special in ordained priesthood, beyond the respect and affection of ordinary human encounters, is evident. Is it respect for the effectiveness of the pastor/priest's activities? Or is it awe at some special measure of Divine Self-presencing? Fundamentally, the pastor/priest—however much pressed by this culture to be defined by *doing* rather than by *being*—is not just a functionary provided "from outside" to teach, preach, direct, and administer, but is to *be there* in the eschatological community, a unique gifting and vocation of *being with (metousiosis)* the Self-presencing God. For us, the meaning of ordination springs, then, from what the pastor/priest is, first, rather than deriving its meaning from the pastor/priest/bishop's activities. If so, then our dialogue in this area might best begin with the *perichoretic*,[6] transfigured reality (see Chapter 9) of the pastor/priest/bishop as a special embodiment of the Triune God in the world. Special indeed. Ordained by God, sacramental.

One Church in One Place

Orthodox and Lutherans arrived in America largely from lands where they were one people and one church: Lutherans from Sweden and Norway, Finland and Denmark, and much of Germany; Orthodox from Greece and Serbia, Russia and Bulgaria, and much of Rumania. In their homelands and villages, there was one church in one place, part of the whole church in every place. It was commonly understood that the church was given to be one from its origin, identifiably the same church in every time and place, with whatever diversities of language, music, or architecture.

But it was not so in their new homeland. Hundreds of religious entities, diverse in name, belief, practices, and organization, lived side by side throughout the land, sometimes ignoring the existence of one another, often in competition

---

[6]Two realities intimately interrelated or mutually permeating as one, e.g., matter and spirit.

with each other. The prevailing spirit of tolerance in this culture not only meant that diversity was acceptable, it could be desirable, even when it meant absence of disciplined attention to truth.

We likewise, Lutherans and Orthodox from many languages and cultures, established our own separate churches around language origins and cultural identities: Greek Orthodox, Danish Lutheran, etc. However, we never intended that to be normative. One church in one place was divinely intended and must be manifested. Apparent division could not be regarded as anything more than interim accommodation to our diverse customs, languages, and cultures, and disregard for the essential, visible oneness of the church was to imperil being the church at all. It was that kind of conviction that led our leaders overseas to take steps resulting in the formation of Faith and Order and the World Council of Churches nearly two generations ago. The same conviction has brought us now into serious dialogue in North America—the commitment to, and vision of a shared life in one church with a common faith, sacramental celebration, and witness—in short, full communion in one church with whatever variations in ethnic customs and regional governances.

It is true that neither Lutherans nor Orthodox have arrived at intended oneness in this new homeland, even within our respective traditions, but neither have we accepted that condition as normal. We are both working at it, internally and with one another. Orthodox ethnic jurisdictions are now linked in a Standing Conference of Canonical Orthodox Bishops in America (SCOBA), and most Scandinavian and German Lutherans have united in the Evangelical Lutheran Church in America, alongside the Latvian and Missouri Synod Lutherans. And we are together engaged in the third round of a dialogue whose aim is eventual full communion. We know that the church is one, within whose Living Tradition differentiation is both possible and reconcilable. So prayed our Lord. So pray we.

The Real of Earth and Heaven

As recently as 1965, there was little contact between Lutherans and Orthodox in North America. We were still strangers to each other. While we had much in common, there was too little shared experience for that to be evident except to a small number of our visionary leaders. When a handful of them met to consider the desirability of an official dialogue, His Eminence Archbishop Iakovos, Primate of the Greek Orthodox Church in North and South America, remarked very pointedly: "Our respective doctrinal positions are harmonious in many ways. Indeed, Orthodox theology is actually closer to the Lutheran than to the Roman Catholic position..."[1] Hardly anywhere is that more evident than in our Orthodox and Lutheran perceptions of the inextricable relationship between matter and spirit, in contrast to a pervasive matter-spirit dualism in our culture and among our religious neighbors. It is a problem that underlies nearly all of our divisions as churches and will have to be attended to before we can take major strides towards union.

The Split World Between Matter and Humankind
The presenting problem is that we live in societies preoccupied with the use of matter. Matter is largely regarded as "there" for human benefit. Scientific research and technolog-

---

[1]Minutes of the Agenda Committee for Lutheran–Orthodox Conversations, Dec. 10, 1965.

ical invention are devoted to making it so: advanced labor-saving devices, increased leisure, more comforts, foolproof securities, larger choices, fewer diseases, longer life, etc. The major political blocs within which most of us live are identified by matter-related names—"capitalist" and "communist"—and invest enormous energies in the preservation and extension of their respective systems for exploiting and distributing matter, for "taking dominion over it."

One complication with seeing matter as merely "useful" to humankind is that it is not only not true, it is also counterproductive. This is not to suggest that the material creation is not of use to us. But preoccupation with use leads to exploitation, reckless expendability, trashing, and dis-usefulness. As has been demonstrated repeatedly, that disturbs, distorts, and precludes an intimate knowing relationship (Hebrew, *yedha*) between human beings and nature so as to make mutual care and shared destiny impossible. That particular orientation, typical of secular humanity, is right in assuming a contingency relationship between humankind and matter, but it is a misplaced contingency. Let me illustrate.

When it is assumed that the material world is merely "there for humankind," the implication is that its meaning is contingent upon the meaning it provides for human beings, that it has little or no place, or purpose, or value of its own. Has it in fact no meaning of its own? If it has not, we are indeed caught in a meaningless existence. Even to participate in meaning for humankind, creation must have some intrinsic value, some integrity, some reality, some objectivity beyond human beings. Just as one spouse can be meaningful to the other only by being fully self, that is, other than the projected wishes of the other, so creation is able to provide meaning for humankind only by being other than humankind or our projected wishes. It is because it is not dependent upon us for what it is or why it is that creation is able to provide meaning for us.

But the deeper problem is that there are different modes of objectivity: one as human-assigned objectification, the other as intrinsic objectivity. Modern technocratic people perceive their material world as an objectifiable "thing" in a split world: "subject" human being and "object" world, related by human choice, not ontologically. We are the perceiving subjects of the at-distance perceived, measured, and modified object. The objectified universe (Descartes) can be compartmentalized, examined, analyzed (Aristotle), and reconstructed according to our designs (Enlightenment). As Joe Sittler once noted, even the "obediently spaced and timed atoms in a controlled mechanism dance their proper steps to an orchestration that man has written."[2] It is an objectification that makes science and technology possible, and, so it appears, knowledge and wisdom irrelevant. Not only was our universe split in two—subject human over against object world—our Western system of thought forsook its holistic, integral mode and became increasingly dichotomous. Self was defined in contradistinction to others, present was opposed to past and future, matter was other than mind or spirit, science as fact was opposed to religion as gullibility, world was opposed to church, and intelligence to belief. Consciously and subconsciously, differences were to be dealt with compartmentally, not interdependently. It was "either–or," not "inter–and," "I–it" rather than "I–thou."

It has not always been so, and need not be. Our ancestors, once called "primitive," dwelt in a unified world. Nature, seasons, gods, creatures, tribe, family, stars, truth, and wisdom were a unified whole. Whether by the sophisticated *armonia* of Pythagoras, the *lykke* of pre-Christian Celts, or the *waconda* of early American Indians, our ancestors had a holistic understanding of life, a kinship with its many parts, a conjoining of individual forces with the whole that made all reality interrelated in an all-encompassing spirituality and destiny. Vignettes of that life-style may still be glimpsed from time to time, as, for example, when the Lakota Indian says

[2]*Dialog*, Vol. III (St. Paul, MN, Autumn, 1964).

"Mitakuye oyasin," all (are) my relatives.[3] In that holistic system, reflection on different values and realities was an important and clarifying dialectical process, with keen interdependencies and complementarities as well as differentiations: I–thou, not I–it; *co*-dominion, not dominion.

Another Divider—in Religion

When nuclear physicist Robert Oppenheimer was asked how he related his work on the nuclear bomb to his religion, he replied, "The gate to my laboratory divides my life: my professional intellectual work is on one side, my religion and family are on the other. I do not mix them." The refusal of renowned scientists at a recent conference of Nobel Laureates to dialogue across disciplinary lines or to discuss moral, political or philosophical meanings of their discoveries, or the reluctance of the "religious" to study and engage in dialogue with the scientific enterprise—these suggest some of the deep rifts of our present dualism.

But my concern here is not so much the chasm between religion and other human experiences, as it is the prevalent matter/spirit dualism within religions and religious communities themselves. Its evidences are everywhere. The Old Testament Hebrews expected a New Jerusalem flowing with milk and honey, far from the sufferings of this earthly life.[4] The first generation of Christians expected an imminent Parousia and entrance into an other heavenly realm. Bunyan's Pilgrim finally escapes the horrors of earthly care, to arrive at a distant Shining Gate. C. S. Lewis's "Perelandra" and "Silent Planet" are spiritual realms far removed from this material world. Ahab, in *Moby Dick*, hopes to but can't escape this evil world even by slaying the great white whale. Most gospel and revival songs presuppose that "the sweet bye and

---

[3]Indeed, in some Native American cultures there were no singular personal pronouns ("I," "me," "my"), only what we regard as plurals ("we," "us," "ours").

[4]With respect to matter/spirit, God/world dualism, Old Testament Hebrews were mixed: for some, God was immanent in lowly nature, e.g., Balaam's ass; for others, God was so "high and lifted up" that they dared not even write or utter God's name.

bye" is far, far away. Matter and spirit are two separate realms: earthy is ungodly, godly is nonearthy. For pietists of every age—Gnostics, Mani, from Augustine's two worlds to contemporary fundamentalists—evil and ungodliness are linked with earthly existence. God, spirit, grace, and heaven are on one side; world, corruption, sin, damnation, and hell on the other. Humankind is by nature (or parental sin) on the side of the worldly, and Jesus Christ (or other supra-human saviours) are sent to rescue us from that corrupt world to the heavenly. The material world, like Paley's watch, made initially by God, turned out to be not good enough and is left to run on its own. Titles of scholarly and popular books perpetuate the mischievous theme: reason *vs.* revelation, creation *vs.* redemption, nature *vs.* grace, works *vs.* faith, profane *vs.* sacred. And there is widespread assurance in much American culture religion, only partly subconscious, frequently fortified by clergy, that the purpose of baptism, church membership, communion, and moral life is to ensure safe passage from an earthy world to a spiritual and heavenly one. *Finiti non capax infinitum* (the finite is incapable of infinity). You have to leave one to enter the other.

If there is indeed such a great gulf between the realms of matter and spirit, and if we accept that dualism, does it mean that this material world and we, so long as we are in it, are forever distanced from the divine realm? Not quite. According to the perceptions of two of the foremost traditions in Western Christendom, either humankind can be gradually "spiritualized" by divine influence (Calvinism) or matter can be instantly "spiritualized" by transubstantiation (Roman Catholicism). Risking over-simplification to the point of caricature, let me illustrate with their respective sacramental practices, sacraments being the interface between the realms of spirit and matter.

In Calvinism, which provides the theological foundation for mainline Protestantism in America (Presbyterians, Reformed, Baptists, Methodists, Disciples of Christ, and large parts of the United Church of Christ), eucharistic bread and wine are and remain ordinary bread and wine. But because of these material "symbols," we remember Christ spiritually and "our souls are fed" spiritually in order that we may be made spiritually one with him. It is the *benefits* of the Eucharist that are important: it is "another aid, near and similar to the preaching of the Gospel, to the sustaining and confirming of the faith."[5] What the objective reality of the elements is is not important. A placebo will do as well as real medicine if the benefits, the gradual spiritualizing of the communicant, are the same. Material and spiritual realms remain separate.

For Roman Catholics the material bread and wine are transformed miraculously into Body and Blood—totally transformed. They are no longer bread and wine, but only have the appearance of bread and wine. What is really present after the consecration is *entirely* Christic—Body and Blood, Christ himself. And "if anyone should say that in the most holy sacrament of the Eucharist there remains the substance of bread and wine *together with* the Body and Blood of our Lord Jesus Christ, … let him be anathema."[6] One substance cannot at the same time bear two realities, earthy and divine. A similar assumption seems to operate in other areas as well. When Mary became the very special bearer of God *(Theotokos)*, she could no longer be regarded as merely human—earthly—with us; therefore Roman Catholics invented the doctrines of her Immaculate Conception and Assumption. When the priest-candidate is ordained sacramentally, he is totally ordained, "indelibly" and transhumanly, and is expected so to conduct himself. When the bridal couple is sacramentally married, the Divine takes over, the couple's relationship becomes as it were transubstantiated, i.e., of a

---

[5]J. T. McNeill, ed., *Calvin: Institutes of the Christian Religion, Vol. 2* (Westminster Press, Philadelphia, PA, 1960), IV, 14, 1 ff. For a brilliant discussion of Calvin's and Calvinists' positions see B. A. Gerrish, *Grace and Gratitude: The Eucharistic Theology of John Calvin* (Fortress Press, Minneapolis, MN, 1992), Ch. 6, "The Mystical Presence."

[6]Council of Trent, 1545–1564. Roman Catholic exceptions to this dualism are found in Dominican and Franciscan spirituality and elsewhere.

divine order, and if the marriage breaks down, re-enters human frailty, it may be annulled as having never been "made in heaven." The natural, material world can be transformed, miraculously, into spiritual reality, but it must be one or the other, not both. In that kind of struggle the human or material components come off at the little end as "accidents." One well-known Catholic theologian has attempted to find an alternative to that kind of dualistic transubstantiation with "transfinalization" and "transignification."[7] In so doing he approaches close to Zwingli's spiritualization, demonstrating again the difficulties of correcting a fundamental spirit/matter dualism, in this case with another spirit/matter dualism. Recent reflections of the Vatican on the World Council of Churches' document, *Baptism, Eucharist and Ministry*, likewise come down approvingly on the Eucharist as a "memorial" celebration.[8]

"En Arche," Where It All Begins

But suppose matter and spirit are not categorically separated realms. Suppose that it is the concern of God, even outside space and time, to be also *in* space and time—earthy and incarnate; not just from way back before when, but continually, perpetually, to be, to have, to inhabit God's creation. This is more than Michelangelo's finger of God, which creates at a distance, from outside; this makes it happen from the inside. Here is where I find colleagues in nuclear physics very helpful.

Werner Heisenberg was one of the great nuclear physicists of this century. Not only a renowned theorist in his explanation of quantum mechanics, his formulation of the Uncertainty Principle, and his quest for a unified theory of all reality, as a

---

[7]Fr. Schillebeeckx, "Transubstantiation, Transfinalization, Transignification" in *Living Bread, Saving Cup: Readings on the Eucharist* (R. K. Seasoltz, ed., Liturgical Press, Collegeville, MN, 1982), p. 189.

[8]*Baptism, Eucharist and Ministry: Faith and Order Paper 111* (World Council of Churches, Geneva, Switzerland, 1982). The document itself, while giving "lip service" to a "memorial" understanding, actually comes down more approvingly of *anamesis* and *mysterion*/sacrament in the Patristic understanding.

gracious renaissance man he delighted in the classic arts, in poetry, philosophy, the natural world around him, and his evangelical faith. I spent part of a sabbatical year with him at the Max Planck Institute for Physics and Astrophysics in Munich a few years ago, and shared some reflections about the connections between theology, philosophy, and physics—that is, about matter and spirit.

As a physicist, Heisenberg leads us down the Comptean ladder of matter, from galaxies, planets, and societies, to persons, molecules, neutrons and protons, subparticles, "swirls of energy" made up of dimensionless nonquarkians and hadrons, which in turn are made up of a combination of three or possibly six preparticles called "quarks," each quark with a corresponding anti-quark. Whether quarks and complementary anti-quarks, or some yet deeper entities occurring in combinations, it is of these combinations that all matter—atoms to galaxies—is made. And that combining and forming, happening constantly *within* the "hard" matter that we perceive, is in Hilbert space, a kind of shadow or pre-space within which ordinary space/time is made, where it might be said that "no-thing" is divided into complementary "things," matter and anti-matter. It is an incredibly busy process,[9] and clearly means that creation was not a once-done-for-always event, but is a perpetual happening, that ours is a constantly "being created" world. Here, at the "bottom," Heisenberg describes a dimension of form, symmetry, and, finally, *Logos* (Word):

> ... there is no longer in the beginning the material object, but form, mathematical symmetry. And since mathematical structure is in the last analysis an intellectual content, we could say ... "In the beginning was the word"—the

[9]Prof. Paul Weiss, in *Mind and Nature* (Univ. Press of America, Washington, DC, 1977), p. 4, calculates that the human brain alone has about 10^{10} cells, that each cell has 10^5 macromolecules, roughly equal to the age of our galaxy measured in seconds. If we can assume that each macromolecule comprises 10^5 quarks, and that each quark has an average life span of 10^{15} seconds, then the entity "turnover" in one's brain in one second would be 10^{35}, i.e., 1,000,000,000,000,000,000,000,000,000,000,000,000 times.

logos. To know this logos in all particulars and with complete clarity with respect to the fundamental structure of matter is the task of present-day atomic physics …[10]

Leon Lederman, recently retired Director of the Fermi National Accelerator Lab in Illinois, conjectures that at the "bottom," as the basic working quarks are coming into existence, there is a mysterious special force—a special quark—that may provide direction and motivation. He calls it the "God particle."[11] By whatever name, "In the beginning (*en arche*, at the bottom, the nadir, the *dabhar*, the beginning before the beginning, where it all starts) was the *Logos* (the Word, the divine act, the creating), and the Word was with God, and the Word was God … All things came into being through him, and without him not one thing came into being" (John 1:1–3). At that moment and that juncture between Hilbert space and time-space, there is some kind of collusion between no-thing becoming and not-quite-yet-some-thing, collusion with the *Logos,* the God particle. In either case Lederman and Heisenberg presume the fact of divine immanence where it all is beginning, is always happening. And the Word doesn't just *make* flesh, the Word *becomes* flesh and dwells among us. Not only is God not estranged from his creation, but, *pan-en-theos,* he is *in* it all, from ground up: "I am everywhere, in heaven and on earth" (Jer. 23:24).

Our methodology at this point comes down to a different way of looking at things. It is to see imaginatively "from the inside." Our normal way is to see from the outside. And what the Heisenberg/Lederman thesis proposes is that the internal reality, the most really real of all matter, is an aspect of God himself—*pan-en-theos* (God in all, not God equals all). There is no being without him, no-thing without his being within it,

[10]W. Heisenberg, M. Born, et al., *On Modern Physics* (Potter, New York, 1961), p. 19.

[11]Leon Lederman, *The God Particle* (Houghton Mifflin, New York, 1993).

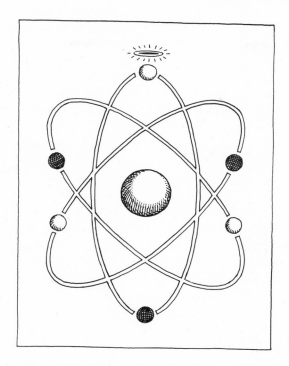

Whether called *"Energeia,"* or "Hand of God," or *"Mysterion,"* or "God Particle," the presence of God is real in all that is.

creating and re-creating it. If that is true, then every meal, every grape, every grain of wheat, every cup of water, every cobblestone not only re-*minds* us of God *(anamnesis)*, but is the "presentness" of God, an aspect of God.[12] And if this is true, it means that every particle of earthy stuff is candidate

---

[12]*An-a-mnesis,* usually translated from Jesus' invitation at the Last Supper (Luke 22:19), "Do this *in remembrance* of me," has a much deeper meaning than mental recollection. As a double negative, a literal translation might be "not ignoring" the Reality always there, namely, Jesus Christ in, with, and under the bread and wine. As Russian Orthodox Professor Vladimir Lossky puts it, "the word *anamnesis* does not mean commemoration simply; rather does it denote an invitation into a mystery, the revelation of a reality which is always present…" *The Mystical Theology of the Eastern Church* (James Clarke & Co., Cambridge, England, 1973), p. 189.

for sacramental union—except that God-in-Jesus set apart very few from very many and made intensive celebration possible, and is at the same time representative of all. It is true, nonetheless, that every meal, every bath, every breath, every word spoken, by virtue of the Divine Reality therein, has a sacramental quality of an analogous sort and should be honored. But a celebrated sacrament is a selected, ordained particularity—the Eucharist is a momentary intersection at which are disclosed and transfigured to one another, God, humankind, and the whole cosmos of God. They there commune together.

Real Presence: The Hand and Energies of God
Ours is not, then, a dualistic world of unrelated matter and spirit. Orthodox and Lutheran thinkers have been adamant about that. The Orthodox have long had several ways of saying that God and matter, though never identical, are nonetheless not "worlds apart." Saints Basil, Gregory Palamas, Athenagoras, and others refer repeatedly to God's proceeding forth as his uncreated *Energeia* (Energies) within everything and outside everything. Indeed "that which has no *Energeia* can in reality have no existence."[13]

(These) *Energeia* are not an intermediary between God and man, not a "thing" that exists apart from God. They are, on the contrary, *God himself,* God in action, God in his self-revelation, ... not a part or division of God, but they are severally and individually the whole God, God in his entirety. Just as the whole God is present without diminution or subdivision in each of the three persons, so he is present entire and undivided in each and all of the divine energies..."[14]

[13]Palamas, *Contra Akindynus,* I, vii, 2, 18. Palamas's published works will be found in J. P. Migne, *Patrologia Graeca* (Migne, Paris, 1857–1866, Vols. 50 and 51).

[14]Palamas, *Triads,* III, ii, 7, *op. cit.* For an excellent introduction to Palamas and *Energeia,* see V. Lossky, note 12, and J. Meyendorff, *A Study of Gregory Palamas* (Faith Press, London, England, 1964).

That means God is present, is real, in all matter, as well as beyond matter. "The Divine Essence is omnipresent, inseparable from its *Energeia*," though we know his Energies, not his Essence.[15]

Luther prefers the psalmist's expression, "hand of God," to describe God's immanence in the created material order:

> It is God who creates, effects, preserves all things through his almighty power and right hand ... For he dispatches no officials or angels when he creates and preserves something, but all this is the work of his divine power itself. If he is to create or preserve it, however, he must be present and must make and preserve his creation both in its innermost and outermost aspects ... Therefore, indeed, through and through, below and above, before and behind, so that nothing can be more truly present and within all creatures than God himself with his power. For it is he who makes the skin ... the bones ... the hair ... the marrow. Indeed, he must make everything, both the parts and the whole. Surely, then, his hand which makes all this must be present; that cannot be lacking.[16]

How do we human beings respond to that divine immanence, to "seeing from the inside"? In one of two ways. Orthodox Prof. Nicolas Zernov sums it up. After noting sadly how Western Christians persist in dichotomizing their world(s)—spirit vs. matter, heavenly vs. earthly, sacred vs. profane—he remarks that Eastern Christians have wondered "how far some of the so-called Low-Churchmen hold the conviction that the lower creation is something inferior which does not deserve to be included in the supreme act of communion between God and man." And then continues: "In all the mysteries of his condescension God approaches

---

[15]Palamas, *Capita*, 74, *op. cit.*

[16]R. Fischer and H. Lehmann, eds., *Luther's Works, Vol. 37* (Fortress Press, Philadelphia, PA, 1983), pp. 58–63.

man from below; and man must be ready to stoop to meet him."[17]

Will(s), Bipolarity, and Perichoresis

One deduction that I extrapolate from Heisenberg/Lederman has to do with the freedom and binding of will(s). As Divine *Energeia* or *Logos* in Hilbert space initiates some kind of thrust towards creativity, a "blister" or node, a pre-quark with the potential of coming into being at the edge of time-space is somehow given the pre-perception of that possibility. At that moment the potentia-to-be already exercises some willingness to be. Then being is on the way to becoming real by the combined will of the Divine and the will of the thing-to-be.

This suggests that for every entity ready to be brought into being, a will of its own is pre-given to it. Divine *Energeia* starts the urge for earthly existence on its way, and at that point the will of the "becoming" joins in.[18] And that will is not just the operative choices of an entity already in being, but the assertion and reassertion towards being of the "becoming" entity; that is, will deals more crucially with *whether* I am than what I decide behaviorally. Will is in this sense *self*-determination before it is moral decision. And when a prospective thing-to-be has no will to be, no drive to survive, no concern for connectedness, no risk for innovation from no-thingness, it will not be. The whole ongoing process of coming-into-being suggests, then, that every particle, from pre-quark to human consciousness, participates in its becoming in terms of both freedom and will. The will of the being-created responds to and cooperates with the divine will in its coming-into-being by exercising its willingness-to-

---

[17]N. Zernov, *The Church of the Eastern Christians* (Macmillan, New York, 1942), p. 100.

[18]Edmund Sinnott in his *Cell and Psyche: The Biology of Purpose* (Harper and Row, New York, 1961) refers to this as the primitive, goal-seeking, upward thrust of life, some collusion involving the material, the biological, and the psychological, a yearning to exist, to be discrete, which is at the very beginning, preconscious, presystemic, developmental. Whitehead calls it "initial aim," God-given; Teilhard de Chardin, "appetancy," an "internal propensity"; Heisenberg, an "isospin directive" related to the inner *Logos.*

be within the possibilities open to it. Human being (and quark) would, in this limited but grand sense, participate in its creation as co-creator.

This continual coming-into-being process then involves, embodies, eventuates in each single and systemic thing as a bipolar reality. One pole is the Divine *Energeia,* the other pole is the thing-will, inseparable from but not identical with *Energeia.* Without *Energeia* there is no-thing. Without each "thing's" self-will there is no-thing. The two relate—coinhere, interpenetrate, mutually indwell perichoretically—to become one space-time thing, or "person." To make application against spirit/matter dualism, divine and nondivine are not fundamentally opposed or contradictory. Therefore spirit and matter are not opposed, nor does spirit become matter or matter become spirit. Nor are they merely contiguous. Divine and nondivine are rather coinherent and mutually inter-extensive. Except both be there and mutually within the other, there is no matter, no creation. Except that coinherence becomes *real,* there is no time-space-history.

To this point we have tried to deal with the objective reality called creation, with ontology. Now we turn to our subjective possibilities of perceiving that reality. That reality, from pre-quark up, is established upon and bears within itself the Divine *Energeia;* it therefore comprises or is comprised by both a divine and a nondivine, or divine-free component or pole. What appears as material stuff, then, is not just a thing-in-itself, but bearer and revealer of something beyond itself, which is at the same time within and fundamental ground *(urgrund)* of itself. That bipolar reality *can* be perceived as mere matter, that is, its divine-free side. Or it can be perceived as the fullness of what it is—with divine embodiment—trans-figured. If the latter, then one can regard the whole creation, including ourselves, as having a quality of sanctity, beyond usefulness, to be respected, cared for, and praised, as "waiting ardently for the revealing of the sons of God" and disclosure of its deeper Reality (Rom. 8:19). Not that the "apparents" of matter are themselves to be praised, but the deeper Reality who has seen fit to participate, to create, to dwell in, and to express himself in this earthy reality. To paraphrase Professor Zernov, it is God who comes to us from below, and we must be prepared to stoop to meet him. But not everyone recognizes him there. One person looks at a painting and calls it a work of art. Another looks at its effect on students and calls it a visual aid. Still another looks and recognizes beyond the colors, lines, and wood the expression of Divine Reality, and calls it an icon—or looks beyond and within bread and wine, and calls it Body and Blood. That is what I mean by "transfiguration" of creation. The Reality is already there; one now sees it differently. I think that is what Heisenberg is talking about—the perichoretic union of matter-spirit. And our fundamental being—a perichoretic union—means that human beings and matter were not cast into time and space unwittingly, fatalistically, and alone, to make whatever we can of it Sartrian fashion. We share with our Creator creation's making and responsibility for it. We also share with creation, not just salvation for human beings, but for the whole cosmos, which is capable of bearing the Divine.

Bread and Wine: Transfigured

What are the implications of that inner *Logos,* of immanental *Energeia* or Hand of God for Orthodox and Lutheran eucharistic bread and wine? Certainly more than symbolic, and certainly different from transubstantiation. One Orthodox theologian remarked to me recently that while we both, Orthodox and Lutheran, dislike the term consubstantiation, that is indeed what we practice. That would mean that eucharistic bread and wine are still bread and wine, but the deeper reality within both is *Logos, Energeia,* Presence of God—"in, with, and under" the bread and wine: "in," as not just external to or transcendent above; "with," as alongside of and not obliterating; "under," as ground and creator of. The really Real is God, *Real* Presence, already there, bodily. In which case a better word for our limited human understanding of this great mystery might be transfiguration, as happened at Emmaus on that first Easter evening, or earlier on Mt. Tabor. Christ as God was already there, but they didn't perceive him as such until his revealing, i.e., transfiguration. Their perception was changed.

Against pervasive dualisms all around him, Luther was a fierce protagonist for the inseparability, though not the indistinguishability, of God and creation, of Father/Son/Spirit, of the two natures of Christ, of the two natures in the Sacrament. Bread and wine are real; Christ's body and blood are real—both *really present* to the faithful believer. There is no place in the Sacrament for dualism, either spiritual (Zwingli) or material (transubstantiation). And that is a mystery beyond explanation, of that Luther was sure.[19]

For Orthodoxy also there is no fundamental dualism between matter and spirit. God and nature are not mutually opposed. By participating in creation, *Energeia* does not replace the naturalness of created matter,[20] but is hypostatically conjoined *with*; the union of Divine *Energeia* and "natural" does not destroy the ongoing reality of the two uniting "natures." By his *Energeia* God is already present in creation, including bread and wine, which, as St. Irenaeus pointed out already in the 2nd century, means that the Eucharist consists of both realities, earthly and heavenly.[21] That does not, however, resolve the problem between immanence in general and Presence in particular, between ordinary *energeic* bread and wine and consecrated Body/Bread and Blood/Wine. A mystery? Assuredly. But if we are uncomfort-

---

[19]See Hermann Sasse's excellent study of Luther on Real Presence, *This Is My Body* (Lutheran Publishing House, Adelaide, South Australia, 1977).

[20]As against, e.g., Apollinaris whose Divine *Logos* replaces the human mind of Christ.

[21]"For as the bread, which is produced from the earth, when it receives the invocation of God, is no longer common bread, but the Eucharist, consisting of two realities, earthly and heavenly..." St. Irenaeus, "Against Heresies," IV, 18, 5, in A. Roberts and J. Donaldson, eds., *Ante-Nicene Fathers, Vol. 1* (Christian Literature Publishing Co., Buffalo, NY, 1885), p. 486.

able with the options of Roman Catholic transubstantiation and Calvinist symbol, perhaps some further steps of clarification could be taken. For example, St. Basil, even before the great liturgist St. John Chrysostom, prays at the Sacrament:

> ...that thy Holy Spirit may come upon us and upon the Gifts here set forth together *(metabalon),* may bless them and consecrate them ... And *manifest* this Bread as the sacred Body itself of our Lord, and God, and Savior Jesus Christ...[22] *(emphasis mine).*

Manifest? Show? Make clear to our perception? The Reality is already there. In the Eucharist, the church is gathered together and has revealed to itself—epiphanically, transfigured—the way things are in God, i.e., all are indwelt by the *Logos.* As Father Alexander Schmemann has said in an unpublished paper, it is not a matter of magic influence on the elements, but a revelation of Christ resurrected and self-presented to us with material things without being imprisoned in them. In which case could not John Chrysostom be translated:

> ... setting forth with *(metabolon)* Thy Holy Spirit, make this bread and that which is in this Cup *be to those who receive them* Body and Blood of Thy Christ... *(emphasis mine).*

As Mircea Eliade puts it, by manifesting the sacred, an object becomes something else, yet continues to remain itself.[23] A sacred stone or tree—or bread and wine—are not worshipped as stone or tree, but because they show something that is no longer seen as merely stone or tree. In the Eucharist, bread and wine, Body and Blood, are revealed to the partaker as present, coming together, as the Council of

---

[22]Still nearer apostolic times, Christians in Syria prayed "...send down Thy Holy Spirit...that He may *show* this bread to be the Body of Thy Christ and this cup to be the Blood of Thy Christ..." Dom Gregory Dix, *The Shape of the Liturgy* (Dacre Press, Westminster Glasgow, 1947), pp. 228, 287, 291. Cf. Cyril of Jerusalem's "...*declare* this bread ... to be ..." Hugh Wybrew, *The Orthodox Liturgy* (St. Vladimir's Seminary Press, Crestwood, NY, 1996), p. 43.

[23]Mircea Eliade, *The Sacred and the Profane* (Harcourt, New York, 1959), pp. 11–13.

Chalcedon explains the two natures of Christ, "in one *prosopon* (person) ... made known to us in two natures, without confusion, change, division or separation." Mutually indwelling, *energeic* bread/Body and wine/Blood are transfigured; perceiving communicants are transformed. How, and how much is in the domain of mystery, celebrated if not rationally comprehended.

One thing that is demonstrated here is that Orthodox and Lutherans have more in common with each other than either has with the dualisms of Calvinism or Roman Catholicism. Still, it may not be as clean as that sounds. There are some Lutherans who are transubstantiationists, some who are Calvinists. There are some Presbyterians who espouse Real Presence, some Catholics who practice Calvinism, and perhaps some Orthodox who would like to rationalize the *Mysterion*. We can still observe distinctions between churches in general, but the existence of variations *within* each tradition accentuates the imperative for extended, in-depth attention to these matters so critical to the exercise of our faith and the uniting of the churches.

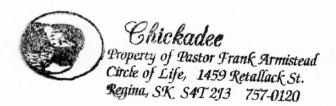

Chickadee
Property of Pastor Frank Armistead
Circle of Life, 1459 Retallack St.
Regina, SK S4T 2J3 757-0120

Roundtables and Courtrooms:
A Question of Style

There's a pair of red-winged blackbirds that make their nest in a fir tree alongside my sweet corn patch. In the spring, when I begin spading the soil and planting the seed, it's not a "no-fly" zone to Mr. and Mrs. Blackbird. Screaming stridently out of the sky, dive-bombing at my hair from all directions, they clearly intend to drive me off. I've had other birds land on my shoulder and wait for a worm to show up in the freshly turned soil. Not these birds. In a few weeks the corn has tasseled. The tassels are obviously expected to provide a landing runway and sturdy perches for Mama and Papa Blackbird. Their landing pattern is steep and fast. In a few days the tree-like tassels are stripped to bare, broken stems. By then, fortunately, many but not all of the silks running to the budding kernels have been pollinated.

Nearer the house a ruby-throated hummingbird seems to float from blossom to blossom, scarcely touching the delicate flower trumpets as it sips nectar, and in the process pollinating the seeds for the next generation. No noise, no bluster. What a style!

My Orthodox hosts in Bulgaria, a bishop from the Holy Synod and a professor from the theological faculty, had invited me to visit the historic, 10th-century Rila monastery in the Rila mountains some seventy-five miles southwest of

Sofia. We had completed the business that brought me to Bulgaria, so now we could enjoy other subjects of common interest, avoiding subjects that might be construed by the driver of the official state car as politically subversive.

Bulgaria has been largely Orthodox Christian, over 80 percent, since the 9th century, with a minority of Muslims left over from Turkish occupation, a few Jews who escaped the Nazis, and a handful of evangelical progeny of Western missionaries. No Lutherans.

"Professor Tobias," the bishop asked, "the only Lutherans we know are those some of us studied with in Germany. Are all Lutherans like that?"

I wondered: like *which* Lutherans in Germany? Perhaps they had studied with Professor Harnack whose description of Orthodoxy was "idolatry"; or with Professor Ritschl who condemned Orthodox mysticism and spirituality as unsystematic, unhistorical, and un-Christian. I had studied with Paul Tillich who escaped from Hitler and was teaching at my seminary in New York. Surely there was hardly any professor so gentle and gracious anywhere in the world. Or did they have in mind the kind of German professors of whom another of my teachers, Professor Kroner, also an escapee from Hitler, said: "How glad I am to be in your country (the U.S.) where men are not in fierce competition with one another. In my country it's every bulldog for himself, and woe to those who don't go along." Or did they mean like the "Tübingen theologians"? In the 16th century, Luther and Melanchthon, when it seemed clear that continuing in the Roman Catholic church was out of the question, were interested in the possibility of developing ties with the Eastern Orthodox church. But Constantinople, key patriarchate of the Orthodox churches, was in Turkish-occupied territory, virtually closed to communication. Nevertheless, a group of Lutheran theologians in Tübingen did succeed in opening correspondence with the Ecumenical Patriarch.

In the course of that correspondence, which began with the most friendly tone and intention, the Tübingen professors pressed their position harder and harder, became more adversarial and strident, at one point declaring that "If they (the Orthodox) wish to take thought for the eternal salvation of their souls, they must join us and embrace our teaching, or else perish eternally."[1] The patriarch's final message was, "Go your own way, and do not send us further letters on doctrine but only letters written for the sake of friendship."[2]

Lutherans and Orthodox in North America have now completed two rounds of dialogue. The subject of the first round's work was primarily a Lutheran agendum. The subject of the second round, justification and *theosis,* was again a Lutheran agendum. During the second round, two of our Orthodox partners spoke with me, distressed with the pushy style of our Lutheran participation. Was it an echo of my Bulgarian host's question: "Are all Lutherans like that?" Also in America? But, then, we could remind ourselves of the irenic Swedish Archbishop Soderblom, or in America of Conrad Bergendoff, whose wisdom and grace make "kinder, gentler" a commonplace, or of our late colleague Joe Sittler. I think that old saw must have been invented for him: if he told you to go to hell (which he wouldn't) it would be with such grace and exquisite language that you'd look forward to the trip.

Two Styles
Among Lutherans there are different styles. Some of us are indeed given to individualism, to polemics, to debate, to cere-

---

[1]Timothy Ware, *The Orthodox Church* (Penguin, New York, 1993), p. 103. Nearly 140 years earlier, a similar "difference of style" thwarted the attempt to reconcile Roman Catholic and Orthodox churches at the Council of Florence. Western Catholics disliked the mystical theological style of the East; Eastern Orthodox were put off by the scholastic systematics of the West.

[2]For a careful documentation and evaluation of that correspondence, see George Mastrantonis, *Augsburg and Constantinople* (Holy Cross Orthodox Press, Brookline, MA, 1982). For a brief evaluation, see Fr. John Travis's paper in Vol. II of the official dialogue report.

The First Ecumenical Council, Nicaea, 325 C. E., condemned Arianism for denying the divinity of Christ, and formulated the Nicene Creed. In the 16th century, Lutherans favored the calling of another genuinely ecumenical council to consider the issues between Lutherans and the Western Roman church, hoping to achieve ecumenical agreement.

brality before communality, to scientific systematics over the mystical and liturgical—overly aggressive to get on with it. It's a style appropriate to the courtroom, hardly the roundtable or altar rail. That has led to heated controversy among us, but also to serious theological research, to rational clarification, to cognitive illumination and much writing—of all sorts. There is also another style, which I associate with the Augustana (Swedish) Lutherans with whom I was first affiliated among Lutherans in America, where theological "knowledge" meant spiritual companionship (Hebrew *yedha*) before it meant scientific systematics and doctrinal purity, where resolution was achieved by familial consensus, not majority vote, after which a common "front" was presented to the outside world. That is a style that I had already learned to associate with Eastern Orthodoxy, a corrective right lobishness in contrast to the dominantly left lobish mode of my own Germanic ethos. But, in the marketplace or the courtroom, whether ecumenical, academic, or whatever, it must be recognized that the irenic, the "kinder, gentler" person will be less visible, and therefore less likely to be put forward as a representative in the public arena. "Nice guys finish last"—or at least are not named to argue the case in court. In the courtroom one presents the best of one's own case, suppresses exceptions, reservations, contraries. The objective is not to present a balanced case for a balanced decision. Right or wrong, win the case. At the roundtable, the objective is to find the wisest solution—all ramifications must be laid out on the table. It's the procedure of the Native American council, not of an adversarial party system. Everyone for the whole truth, not just "our side" of the case.

There's no denying we have a real contrast of style here, perhaps a conflict in the souls of all of us. Even in the shaping of this book we are torn between the drive to be precise, systematic, and scientific (in the technological, not the Greek philosophical sense). Concerned with facticity, with dates, sites, and numbers on the one hand; with values, qualities, and interrelationships that transcend time, numbers, and places on the other. It is my Germanic genes in contest with my Indian spirit! So, also, however caricatured, is the difference in style between Lutherans and Orthodox: Lutherans

first seeking accuracy—never mind what that does to relationships—and then accord; Orthodox seeking, no, not
seeking, *practicing* wholeness, within which accord and accuracy are realized. And that problem, the problem of style, is
likely to be the most difficult between us in our North
American dialogue, as also within the Lutheran family itself.
As Lutherans, we need urgently to address that, and I
suspect one of the good ways we might begin is to review
that ancient way of our Celtic forebears, the roundtable,
which was going strong long before the advent of the adversarial courtroom and Roman legal debates. Another assist
may come from remembering that it is Incarnation that is and
must be the melding together of the discrete historical and
the eschatological eternal, of minute facticity and cosmic
quality, of matter and spirit. Differences in style? Or complementarities of styles? That is a matter we must attend to.

No, your Grace, not all Lutherans are like the aggressive
systematicians you met in Germany. There are Lutherans in
Scandinavia, Africa, Latin and North America, and also in
Germany (remember the Confessing Church?) as well as
among Native Americans who would be quite at home in an
Orthodox ethos: mystical, liturgical, communal, holistic—yet
not without concern for doctrinal clarity and truth. But if you
have only limited contacts with Lutherans, the ones you are
most likely to meet are the same kind you met in Germany,
the Harnacks, the Ritschls, the Scholastics.

As our car hair-pinned up into the Rila foothills, leaving the
villages and farms of the fertile valleys, we came to vast
groves of young evergreens. Here was a prized achievement
of the young Communist government. For centuries, especially during invasions and occupation by the Turks, the
Orthodox Bulgarian villagers, as throughout the Balkans,
were forced to convert, or to flee to the hills, or to die. Most
fled to the hills. Shepherding became their way of life. The
people survived, but the slopes were eventually nibbled
nearly to bare rock. With rains came erosion, floods, barren-

ness. Now the shepherds and flocks had been moved down to the valleys and plains. The young trees again showed promise of restoring the foothills and forests, even the mountains, for future generations. The young people who planted the trees were very proud of their work. Their elders, the shepherds, who were forced to take up dirt farming in the plains below, were distressed. Any change of life-style can be distressing; for these shepherds, who weren't accustomed to being pushed, it was especially traumatizing, and will continue to be so until the next generation can begin to enjoy the results: no more flash floods, cooler summer breezes, water reservoirs and trickling trout streams, restored wildlife and parks, eventually lumber and paper products.

Our conversation—that of the bishop, the professor, and I—turned to theology, what it is, what it does, who does it. In the Orthodox church the bishop is respected as a theologian. That doesn't mean he is university trained in the science of theology, but he has spent time as a theological student, as a priest in a parish, and as a monk in a monastery,[3] has read and breathed the atmosphere of the church's Fathers and theologians, and is concerned that a consensus be reached after all opinions are heard. That qualifies him for the theological business of the Orthodox church, that is, he is the mentor, arbiter, and Solomon on theological matters. In the Lutheran tradition it is the theological professors who adjudicate theological matters.[4] There's a difference in objective, in method, and in result. In the Lutheran tradition the purpose of theological work is to establish what is true and to teach it *(kataphatic)*. In the Orthodox tradition the function of

[3]Lutheran bishops have normally spent four years in graduate seminary and internship, at least three years as parish pastors, and in many cases some years as professors in theological seminaries.

[4]That may change as Lutherans' experience of bishops and Lutheran bishops' experience of "bishopping" mature. After all, American Lutherans have had their own bishops for only eight years, and it may take some time to move from presidents as "chief executive officers" to *Catholicos*—the spiritual/theological link between local parishes and synods, and the whole Church Universal.

theology is to prevent heresy *(apophatic)*—to appreciate the mystery, the "unknowingness" of God. And that means a very different way of going about it: whether to control, shape, and direct the faith on the one hand, or to permit, observe, and remedy responses to the Spirit on the other.

Style! Reconciling these differing accents, beginning with style and differing attitudes toward the relationship between ideas and persons, may take us a very long time.

Mystery and Theology

On the south side of the Rila range, where the mountains slide down into the Aegean Sea, a few miles southeast of Salonica, there's a small village called Stagira. It's a place where we should erect a lofty monument to one of our unnamed patron saints. By "we," I mean scientists and theologians. The patron saint would be Aristotle. Stagira was his native village. Or perhaps at Pella, a few miles west of Salonica, or Athens might be better. Well, maybe not Athens. That's where Aristotle was first a disciple of Plato (367–347 B.C.E.), and later returned as a teacher (335–322). The gardens of Plato's Academy are still there, but no buildings. The old olive tree that provided shade for Plato's discourses with his students was "done in" a few years ago when a bus didn't make the curve in the ancient Holy Way from the Parthenon to Eleusis and Delphi, smashed through the garden wall, and sheared off the main trunk—probably 3,000 years old. There's a new sprout pushing up from the old roots, very tenderly cared for, but it's no place to add further risk with a big monument.

Pella would probably be the right place. That's where the royal palace of Philip of Macedonia stood, where his son Alexander the Great was born and from which Alexander launched his campaigns to reunite Greece and reconquer most of the Middle East from the Black Sea to India and

Egypt. Aristotle was his teacher. The fortifications and walls of the palace have long ago disappeared, probably for construction of St. Paul's Berea some miles to the southwest. Over the centuries the courtyards were buried under sediment and eventually turned into grain fields. Archeologists are presently excavating the vast palace site, and have uncovered beautiful mosaic floors and markings of a great city. There is plenty of space in the surrounding plains for an appropriate monument—a towering spire and extensive labs to signal and facilitate the human quest for the reaches of ultimacy.

But why Aristotle? And why theologians? There was a time when theology was the "queen of sciences." That was before "science" became scientific, when "science" meant to know the "what," the "who," and the "why," not just the "how" of life and the cosmos. Aristotle was that kind of scientist. He was indeed a careful observer of everything around him, but also had a keen passion for digging deeper and deeper until he got to the bottom of things, bit by bit, part by part, piece by piece, then putting it into a total descriptive picture of his world, category by category. Observer, organizer, clarifier, meticulous systematician—patron saint of scientists and Western-style theologians. It's a methodology that has made Western "scientific" thought possible, including the tools for "dominion" over the earth. The Schoolmen of the Middle Ages bought into it and passed it on, including to Western theologians. It was fundamentally a conceptual, propositional, heady, rational process, bent on running down, uncovering, and establishing the verities of God and faith with *summas* and dogmatics and systematics, often heedless of what that did to broader meaningful relationships. In this pursuit for—even completion of—great systems, what happened to the dynamics of meaningful relationships and mysteries and surprises?

In college, my professor of theology had it all worked out. It was a foolproof system from Genesis 1, creation, through

Revelations 22, the final Holy City. Everything was fitted into place, from the Fall to the parting of the waters, to the conditions for salvation, from sex and procreation to the great Armageddon, to hells below and heavens above. Like Thomas Aquinas and the scholastics before him, everything fit appropriately into the total system, the *Summa Theologica*. Whatever was to be known about God was packaged, ready for delivery.

But something didn't seem quite right about that. It was too cut and dried. What happened to mystery and spiritual surprises? To God? The professor wanted our belief to be in the system. Despite his "complete" system, my inquiring mind didn't stop inquiring with his system. Nor did Aristotle's with his. In his later years, Aristotle wrote that "The more I find myself by myself and alone, the more I have become a lover of mystery (myth) ..." Beyond the rational, scientific endeavors of his early years, now he found in quiet contemplation something of a deeper vision of the Divine. And Thomas Aquinas, having completed his systematic *Summa,* which was supposed to tie it all together in a neat theological system, after some kind of vision at the altar one day, asserted of the intellectual system that he had struggled so long to pull together, "It's all so much straw." He laid it aside for contemplative participation in the Divine.

In the West, we construct our elaborate systems—theologies of worship, of evangelism, moral theology, pastoral theology, historical theology, liberation theology, Black theology, feminist theology, systematic theology. At our seminary we even renamed our systematics department "constructive theology." Logical, consistent, noncontradictory conceptualities—it's teachable that way, as a collection of data, but does it climb us up to God? Or bring God down to us?

At the end of World War II I found myself stumbling through the rubble and tragedy and pain of West and East Europe. So much of the elegance and order and beauty and aspirations

"The more I find myself ... alone, the more I have become a lover of mystery"—Aristotle (Spada Gallery, Rome, from a Greek original; adapted). In Orthodoxy, the Eucharist is called the *Mysterion*.

of great cities and great peoples and cultures were crashed down—and so came down my neat system of romantic dreams and ideals of creating a perfect world just beyond the horizon, if we could think and work deeply and clearly and consistently enough. Crash. Tragedy. And mystification. We thought we could storm heaven. But God and heaven are not provided by neat systems. Yes, Aristotle could dissect the butterfly, put names to all its parts, explain how it flies and migrates back to its equatorial home. It's important to be thorough and consistent, but the "complete" system doesn't make the butterfly fly. Systems alone are not enough. So why any kind of disciplined theology?

In East Europe, their war wasn't over. Totalitarian Com–munists were still in control: police state, "big brothers" in every block, five- and ten-year compulsory plans, all-pervasive economic and cultural systems. It was in effect the projection of another Western rational system, foreign to the East, projected onto the East. In the midst of that I was shown another alternative to "systematic," "constructive" theology, Western style. My host bishop and the professor called it *apophatic* theology. It's done a different way, by different people and with different results than most theology in the West.

Participation in Mystery

Theology, Orthodox style, begins with a mystery to be partic-ipated in rather than a problem to be solved. For theological problem-solving, the Western-style theologian must keep a cool, dispassionate distance from the work in progress. Here, we could suggest that Western theologians might well raise up a second monument, perhaps in France, to the famous French philosopher René des Cartes. One thing Descartes was noted for was this keep-your-distance factor. The scien-tist, or teacher, or theologian must stay cool, not get emotionally involved, maintain "objectivity" from the object under examination. That was the only way to arrive at accu-rate, objective solutions. But, when the "object" is a mystery, some numinous, awe-inspiring, unlabeled reality, one begins to know it, or him, by participation. *Yedha*, the Hebrews called it, knowledge, as in intimate intercourse ("and Joseph *knew* her not" Matt. 1:25), not experienced at a cool, rational distance. Martin Buber helps us at this point: we are met with an "I–thou" situation, not "I–it." It is much more than a bag of data. Participation, closer even than partnership. As Augustine observed in one of his better moments: "God is closer to me than I am to myself." Like a deer after water brooks, the true theologian "panteth" after mystery, not just to know its size and doings, but to know its reality, its being, not merely by observing, but by mutual participation—a tryst of awe and love.

There are some wondrous surprises, but also some very grave risks, in that kind of encounter theology. Like Scrooge's mystery encounter in Dickens's *Christmas Carol,* how can one be sure that what appears to be Marley's ghost isn't just a hallucination from an underdone potato? Orthodox theology has some safeguards here. Though not absolutely fail-safe— even in participation and self-revelation it is the mystery God alone who is absolute, not propositions *about* him or experiences *of* him—there are safeguards to reduce the risk of going astray.

One safeguard in Orthodox theology is that it is a community affair. If in the West, theology is the business of individual scholars, worked out in their private laboratories, then published and debated adversarially in the marketplace, in Orthodoxy the culmination of theology is in the whole eschatological community—past, present, future—whose mystery encounters are reported and passed around in Scriptures, creeds, writings of the church fathers and decisions of councils, and in sermons and liturgy. There is indeed disciplined work by specialists in that vast body of messaging, but it is the mentors of the contemporary church, the bishops, who referee the coursing of that process, and who articulate provisional findings along the way. Even if or when a professional scholar does his or her own piece of individual research and writing it is aimed at representing the common mind of the whole church, and not some personal hobby-horse of the writer.

Preventing Heresy
Secondly, in that process, it is the business of theology to remove or prevent error, not to *create* spiritual truth, that is, it is *apophatic* (negative, i.e., not operating with overwhelming proofs). Whereas theology cannot *guarantee* spiritual life, it can prevent disease. In that sense, theology's task is hygienic, preventive, not *kataphatic* (by compulsion, as in macho!). It may clear away hindering thickets, may describe what

the church experiences of Mystery, but it does not create encounter-knowledge by rational systems. Theology may even enable us to press our human possibilities to awareness of their final limits, e.g., Kierkegaard's "abyss," whereby the Mystery God may more readily get through to us. But theology doesn't package or give us God; it is only God who gives God.

From there on, with as clean an encounter field as possible, Orthodox theologizing intends to let the Spirit flow freely, in participation, in knowing, in celebrating, and announcing, and that leaves an openness both for deeper participation and for ever more lively and fresh interpretation. Orthodox theology, therefore, is not long on systems, or schematizations of ideas *about* God, as though such systems could bind and deliver or demonstrate or prove the existence and behavior of God. Yes, they do have a few Western-style theologians (as Lutherans have a few Orthodox types), and they do have one fixed creed, the Nicene-Constantinopolitan, and some confessions addressed to local heresies, but even the universal Nicene Creed was created to say "no" to a major heresy by saying "yes" about the church's fundamental experience of the Holy Trinity.

If theology does not deliver God, does it deliver Truth? But what is truth? In the West, truth has tended to be identified with the accumulation of noncontradictory data, of verifiable, repeatable, compatible correspondences between appearances, events, data, and concepts. Is it "true" (a Western mind asking) that in Orthodoxy Truth is not a collection of logical propositions and conceptual conclusions that by virtue of their noncontradiction are correct, i.e., "true," but that Truth is a matter of unbroken (*aletheia*—nonriven) relationship, in particular with God? If so, then Truth enfolds mysteries, relational mysteries of a God who is both revealed and hidden, mysteries about whose fullness no human has final or absolute claim. In such relational truth there is always some mystery beyond comprehension and participation. Does that imply that from person to person and from time to time there may be variations, and enlargements, not just fixed texts and propositions? That it didn't all happen 2,000 years ago but is still happening, that some things can be different and still equally true? If so, it would mean that Truth is a holistic complex of interrelationships, to be shared, celebrated, worked at, communicated, probed, clarified, enriched, but never finalized. As in marriage, so with Truth, relating precedes and surpasses every attempt at logical description of it. And that brings us again to that intriguing discussion between Pontius Pilate and Jesus: "What is truth?"—Jesus the Eastern theologian of mystery relationships, and Pilate the Western Roman systematician (John 18:38).

God-for-Us

Ah, yes, but there is a *kataphatic* side of Eastern theology, not to construct foolproof systems of propositions and answers, but to encourage all humans everywhere to join in the great tryst between the Almighty Mystery that is God and the fascinating manifestations of his Presence in and hopes for us and this cosmos. When we know we are before something great and mysterious, about which we know enough to know that it has an inner nature we cannot penetrate, that it, rather he, has made that known to us, there we pause—to acknowledge, to confess, to celebrate, but not to conclude, "finality." In old Teutonic, to wonder means to wander, to turn aside from what is great and awesome. But it is not to stay turned away. What we can stay away from is no longer great for us. No. From what seems to be for us Ultimate Mystery we wander, we hide for a while, but we come back again to test whether he is still the Great and the Mysterious. To do less would mean to have given up his being God-for-us. Aristotle, in the end, was a "lover of mystery." And beyond that, conscientiously explored, is not a problem solved, but deeper, richer Mystery.

And so the Bulgarian bishop, the professor, and I concluded our discussion about Lutheran and Orthodox theology. Our car crossed the divide and we came into the valley of Rila monastery. Strangely, young Communists, also on their pilgrim way to a new society, intermingled with monks and religious pilgrims in the calm of ancient cloisters. Down the nearby slopes to the south were the Aegean Sea and Aristotle's birthplace. Nearby is the renowned peninsula of Mt. Athos. I wondered what Aristotle would have made of these great centers of monastic life and contemplation. "The more I find myself by myself and alone, the more I have become a lover of mystery ..." Lutheran theology in its infancy was very close to Orthodox-style theology.[1] In its scholastic middle age it may be complementary but different in many respects from Orthodox theology. Could it be that in its mature years Lutheran thought might, like Aristotle's, find a healthier balance of systematic and mystery theology without creating a serious rift within the Lutheran theological community?

[1] It may at some points even have gone beyond Orthodox *apophasis,* with Luther's categorical *solas,* his deprecation of reason as "the white devil's whore,"and his prescription for a time of excessive legalism: "Love God and do as you please."

Heaven on Earth

We were staying at the modern, high-rise Kosmos Hotel in the northern suburbs of Moscow. It was the mid-1980s. I had brought a seminar of theological students and young pastors for an introductory exposure to Eastern Orthodoxy and to life in a Communist culture. Centered in the huge traffic circle in front of the hotel was that heroic monument to space flight, so dramatically executed that it has been copied in Geneva and other parts of the world. On beyond were the grounds of the permanent and extensive world trades exposition. Impressive, like many things in the former Soviet Union, "bigger than life." In the several square blocks behind the hotel was what at first appeared to be an abandoned dump yard, overgrown with weeds, scattered tin cans, some rusted car parts, crisscrossed here and there with dirt paths. In the far corner, at an intersection a fifteen-minute walk from the hotel through the brush and dirt paths, was an Orthodox church, surrounded by a low-walled churchyard enclosing many graves, some marked with flowers, fresh or browned with age, and some with tombstones. It occurred to me that, as with the grounds around the theological seminary in Leningrad (St. Petersburg), the whole surrounding area, including the grounds under the hotel, was once part of a major monastery set on the pilgrimage route between the inner city of Moscow and the great religious center of Zagorsk, a three-day journey by horse to the northeast. Now those monastery grounds have been nationalized for what are alleged to be much more important uses, except for the church and cemetery.

The severe reduction of monastery lands and monasteries was not the only loss suffered by the Russian Orthodox Church through Communist nationalization and war losses.[1] Between 1917 and 1945, churches and chapels were reduced from 71,457 to 9,225, monasteries from 1,026 to 38, seminaries and theological academies from 62 to 2, church hospitals and welfare institutions from 1,450 to 0, priests from 50,960 to 5,665, and believers from 100 million to 60 million. In the same period, Roman Catholic and Uniate believers stayed even at 6 million, while Baptist, Evangelical, and Pentecostal members increased from 1 million to 4 million, and their church buildings from 500 to 2,000. Orthodox church treasuries were largely confiscated, and precious icons were brought in from chapels and churches throughout the land to be "restored and preserved." From the Bolshevik Revolution (1917) right through the last days of the Soviet KGB, undercover agents were frequently seen at services, presumably to observe who was attending and to ensure that no "subversive activity" was being fostered by the churches. It was enough to make clergy and worshippers at times nervous, and on occasion to be subjected to questioning, punishment, and sometimes death.

It was nearly dark, time for evening Vespers. We made our way down the slippery path, through the darkened dump yard and brush to the church. Once through the door, we entered a different world. Hundreds of prayer candles sparkled brightly before the icon of Mary Theotokos and the iconostasis. More were added as believers moved in and out.

---

[1]See R. Tobias, *Communist-Christian Encounter in East Europe* (School of Religion Press, Indianapolis, IN, 1956), Ch. III and pp. 221–302. Russian Orthodox Patriarch Alexis II reports that during the "process of renaissance" following Communist control in Russia (1988), the numbers of Orthodox parishes have increased from 6,893 to 15,985, priests from 6,674 to 12,841, dioceses from 67 to 117, and bishops from 75 to 139. *Episkepsis* (Centre Orthodoxe du Patriarcat Oecumenique, Geneva, Switzerland, Oct. 31. 1995), p. 4.

The sanctuary was already filled with the incense of prayers offered to the Triune God. The voices of priests, deacons, and lay readers chanting and reading the Scriptures, Psalms, and prayers reverberated in the dimness of the lofted ceiling. Mosaic frescoes and icons reflected light back to us from distant walls and arches, the Almighty Christ looking down rather sternly from the cupola. The worshippers, mostly elderly women but even a few Russian soldiers, were dressed in anything but Easter finery. It was clearly a moment that took much determination—there were after all some risks involved—but it also appeared to be a victorious moment for the worshippers.

I remembered a visit some time earlier to the elegant royal cathedral, I believe it was of the Annunciation, nestled among other cathedrals in the heart of the Kremlin. The cathedral was converted to a national "museum" early in the Bolshevik conquest. The icons were still there, the glorious mosaics, and the tombs of the royal families. But no candles, incense, choirs, or clergy. After we entered I noticed that most of the men, from their clothing I guessed them to be Russian, upon entering removed their hats (the cathedral was as cold as a frozen meat locker). Many walked to the iconostasis, paused, quickly crossed themselves, and left. By then I felt well enough acquainted with our Intourist guide for a bit of teasing. "Tanya, why do the men remove their hats on entering this museum?" "Because they are gentlemen and because there's a sign inside the door requesting gentlemen to remove their hats here in the museum," she replied. Her smile betrayed our shared recognition that there were darker political reasons, and not a little defiance in the men's behavior.

Back to Vespers: as we stood in the nave of the church, some of us occasionally crossing ourselves along with other worshippers, we must have seemed a strange lot to the Russian worshippers around us: brightly colored clothing properly pressed, pink faces scrubbed sterile, hair coiffed Western style, for the most part taller than our "hosts," frequently whispering among ourselves about what was being read or sung, or to ask where they were now in the service. Orthodox believers were not entirely unaccustomed to strangers in their midst who didn't quite keep pace with what was going on: Communist government agents observing who attended, an occasional group of curious Western or Eastern tourists, would-be proselytizers from Western-related sects.

An elderly *babushka* (I mean that as respectfully as I would of my own mother) brushed past us as she was leaving, muttering half under her breath, in Russian, "What are you people doing here? What do you want?" One of our students had studied in Leningrad and knew Russian. Immediately she caught up with the perhaps offended believer, and spoke to her quietly in Russian: "I'm sorry if we've offended you. We've come to worship God with you." Surprised and obviously greatly moved, the woman threw her arms around Melaney: "Oh, you are so welcome." Whatever our clumsiness in the context of other languages and ways of doing things, even sometimes escorted by despised government functionaries, that was most reassuring, and maybe that simple, unconditional heart-to-heart oneness before God can set the tone for our future sharing.

That does not mean we should neglect the very serious attention needed on some doctrinal matters by theologians. But given the variations in our cultural experiences and histories, our styles and ethoi, the key will be to develop a broad-based life together. And that means every aspect of churchly life, especially among the congregations and faithful, that is, to become part of, and welcomed as part of each other's families. "You are so welcome." So, now to comment on some very practical matters for us here in North America, first pertaining to some theological issues where "we already have more in common" than either of us has with our other dialogue partners, and then on to one or two suggestions for developing life together.

On the Theological Front

The second round of our dialogue in North America has done very significant work on the subject of justification and theosis.[2] Some different emphases were recognized in that process: Lutherans place more emphasis on the means of salvation, Orthodox on the meaning of salvation; Lutherans on the "how," Orthodox on the "what" of salvation. Lutherans want to fine-tune how it is that God triggers the process of salvation; Orthodox focus on the consequential life of the saved. Lutheran concern with the sacrifice on the cross inclines them to emphasize "Christ *for* us"; Orthodox concern with the resurrection and continuing Presence inclines them to emphasize "Christ *in* us." Yet each of these accents is claimed as real and true by both, nor do the differences in accents derive from factors inherent in our relations with one another. Further attention to our respective histories will doubtless clarify how these different accents developed out of our encounters with different cultures or heresies, e.g., Lutherans in their formative period responded to a context of "works"—the how of salvation: indulgences, acceptance/rejection social patterns, etc.—therefore came the Lutheran concern for a more appropriate "how." Orthodox, in Greece, Russia, and the Near East, lived in and dealt with a context of mythologies, heavenly deities, and deifications. Therefore came their accent on deification, the "what" of salvation. We may find unexpected harmonies in exploring these cultural factors as related to our central theological issues.

Our respective perceptions of unity, and the nature and function of Ecumenical Councils and confessions received serious but not extensive attention in round two of our dialogue.[3] These three areas may need more detailed attention in the distant future, but work to date has laid sufficient ground of understanding to carry us forward as we attend to some

[2]Reported in J. Meyendorff and R. Tobias, eds., *Salvation in Christ, Vol. I* (see Introduction, note 7).

[3]Reported in J. Meyendorff and R. Tobias, eds., *Salvation in Christ, Vol. II* (see Introduction, note 1).

more urgent matters. When we come back to these areas, it will likely need to be in the broader context of ecclesiology and eschatology, that is, the nature of the church and the nature of time in relation to the church and eternity.

On the Spirituality Front

Styles of spirituality are so deeply embedded in our histories, our cultures, our psyches, that one doesn't jump superficially from occidental to Eastern spirituality, or vice versa. Nowhere in our life is self-integrity more essential than here at the core of our being. However, exposure to other spiritualities and mutual participations at whatever beginning level can be illuminating and deepening. It has been our custom in the Lutheran-Orthodox Dialogue for the host traditions or institutions to conduct worship according to their respective traditions. One morning after Orthodox Matins one of our Lutheran participants remarked, "I was glad to be present as an observer. But I wasn't worshipping." That was early in our sessions together. By the end of our eight years together I think he would have said that he was glad to *worship* with the Orthodox, a new level not only of ecumenical understanding but of divine presencing.

If in our dialogue to date we have focussed on the how and what of God's grace and the consequences, for us, of God's grace—forgiveness, justification, restitution, sanctification, theosis—what about *causes* of God's grace? Would it be too impertinent to want to explore the *why* of God's grace? We have customarily assumed that God's intent was to do something *to* us or *for* us, for *us*. Granted, something tremendously important has happened to us and for us by God's grace and incarnation, but was the benefit we received first of all the *reason for*, or the *result of* God's action? What "salvation" says about *God* is surely no less important than what it says about our human condition. Otherwise, Christology does indeed become soteriology, a crippled soteriology at that.

What if there is something about God himself that makes God want to be alongside, with, and in us? What if there is some-

Greek Orthodox Church of St. Sofia, 6th century, Constantinople (Istanbul). Minarets were added later by Turkish Muslim occupiers. Russian Prince Vladimir's envoys reported, "We didn't know whether we were in heaven or on earth."

thing about God that made him wish for a creature "in his image," with his own nature, capable of companionship with him? What if there is something about God that makes God want to come among us as one of us? What if there is something about the nature of God himself, the all-powerful monarch who can create, who from his throne can topple empires and stay disaster, who in his own being wants to stand by us, to dwell with us, to accompany us *(com-panio,* take bread with us) because of what he is like as much as, even more than, what we think benefits us? "For God so loved the world ..." It's not that the world is so lovable, as that God is so loving, and because he is so loving, God finds the world lovable. And if that's the *why* of incarnation, how would that affect our worshipping, our praying, our daily tasks?

For one thing it would mean that prayer is not to harangue God to "be there," as though he weren't already "there," to plead for things as though he withholds blessing until we beg, to pray as though he doesn't know or doesn't care about our human plight without our informing and instructing him. Worship and prayer in the context of God-already-with-us (Emmanuel) would be a conversation of thanksgiving, of sharing concerns, of broadening and deepening two-way comprehension ("Be ye perfect"—*teleioi,* all comprehending —"as your Father in heaven"), receiving illumination or insight from God while joining with him in his concerns and care of the cosmos. Impertinent? Perhaps. Also profoundly humbling, if it centers us on God and not ourselves. It's part, even if not always articulated that way, of our shared spirituality. And it might even make us a bit more "in his likeness."

Some Challenges, and Fullness
Immanence and transcendence: I come back to this again only to emphasize that in this culture, which races pell-mell towards wider and wider separation of matter and spirit, no two religious communities are more able to bring balance and sanity to such a profound theological and social problem. Human aspirations for peace, for racial understanding, for economic sharing, for fulfilled life, for heaven on earth will be illuminated by rigorous attention to the relation of matter and spirit, behind which is the inseparability of divine immanence and transcendence.

Sacramentality, historic continuity, ordination of women— difficult issues. And yet, Lutherans have not excluded ordination as one of the church's sacraments; we just haven't quite figured out what that means. Orthodox, in historic practice and the expressed opinion of a recent Ecumenical Patriarch, have not definitively excluded ordination of qualified women for specific ministries, and, contrary to the impression of some Protestants, do already include women in significant leadership positions. As to historic continuity, Orthodox theologian John Zizioulas, in his *Being As Communion,* describes apostolic continuity and succession in terms that every catholic-minded Lutheran would welcome.[4] And in fact, those of us in the Augustana (Swedish) and Finnish Lutheran traditions have never intentionally broken our own historic succession in the episcopacy, even if we do not lean heavily on that for apostolic continuity. So it's not inconceivable that we could work these issues out.[5]

Council, Canon, and Confession

One advantage we have today that was lacking when the 16th-century Jeremias-Tübingen correspondence broke off is our common language and face-to-face contact; also there is some flexibility in understanding important if not quite immutable historic events. The Lutheran Confessions, for example, were not originally designed as prescriptive rules for a new Western church. They were intended to describe to the emperor what this new movement was about. In that spirit, when detailed passages in the Confessions are questioned by contemporary Lutherans, or others, they can be interpreted in the context of that era, without denying the working of the Spirit among those reformers, or us. Further, when the church fathers at Nicaea in the 4th century determined that all bishops should memorize all the Psalms, it was assuredly an appropriate decision. What bishop, riding a donkey, could carry several heavy volumes of hand-lettered Psalms and other Scriptures on his rounds among widely scattered parishes? But what church father, debating the memorization canon at Nicaea, would have imagined that all the Psalms could one day be printed in a vest pocket booklet! That particular canon we honor for its timeliness—then; but I don't expect my bishop to memorize all the Psalms (however spiritually illuminating! I do expect him and the rest of us to read them). What I think we can hope for is that such matters

[4]John Zizioulas, *Being As Communion* (St. Vladimir's Seminary Press, Crestwood, NY, 1985), Ch. 5.

[5]Even the Lutheran Church of Denmark, which a generation ago avoided participating with Swedish and Finnish Lutheran churches in ordination services lest they be contaminated with the "historic episcopacy affliction," has recently indicated openness to accepting a historic episcopate. *Baptism, Eucharist and Ministry, Faith and Order Paper 149* (World Council of Churches, Geneva, Switzerland, 1990), p 84.

will be reviewed and updated by the whole church in periodic councils, and guided by the same Spirit. That, I believe, is an appropriate aspect of Living Tradition, at work. The ongoing attention being given to the *filioque* (that the Holy Spirit proceeds from the Father *and the Son*, added to the Nicene Creed by the Western church) may be a case in point, and is under review.

How do we now, Lutherans and Orthodox, work through our diverse externals to deeper levels of shared life? Some study materials, a handbook for persons of all ages, would help. The Dialogue commission is working on that. Some shared pilgrimages, festivals, and forums can be offered eventually, visitations among congregations and lay study groups, guest representation at each other's conventions and assemblies. Some of this is already happening. What is urgently needed are qualified pastors and priests, fully knowledgeable in both traditions and able to interpret the details of our respective traditions in accurate and meaningful ways, perhaps even in some emergencies to be able and qualified to stand in for one another. That will mean some travel, visitation, exchange students and courses at seminaries, and mixed clergy conferences. One idea whose time may have come is to join with the Ecumenical Patriarch in Constantinople in reopening Halki as an international center, including an Orthodox-Lutheran training program for a cadre of younger clergy: a crash course in both traditions, field studies in early church history, including the sites and writings of St. Paul and the Ecumenical Councils, biblical Greek, worship—all of that in a culture sufficiently distant and different to stimulate fresh insights on the American scene and our mission in it. It's an idea we tried a decade ago, but we ran short of money. And now? It's a challenge I hope readers, particularly students and laity, will be ready to grasp and press forward. Or, if not an international center at Halki, perhaps a jointly sponsored institute for shared research, study, training, and worship, possibly at a seminary or monastery somewhere on this continent? In the meantime, far-seeing seminaries can develop curricula and student/ faculty exchanges (some already have) for a "fullness of the church" ministry.

Finally, the prospects of a shared life between Orthodox faithful and Lutheran faithful, of congregation with congregation, will not be easy and cannot be hurried. If we leap too quickly, without adequate preparation, our different styles and externals may fascinate some, but may scandalize many others. If attempted more patiently (hummingbird style!), that can be done along with shared exploration of the roots and meanings of the core of our religious life, where we have not only much in harmony, as Archbishop Iakovos pointed out, but where we may also discover our enormous gifts for each other. In any case, thanks to our gracious God, our wayfaring together is not only thinkable and possible. It has already begun.

As I crossed a moor —

An eagle-feather...

Together.

Detail of a fresco in the monastery of St. Panteleimon,
Nerezi, Macedonia, adapted.

About the Author

Robert Tobias is Emeritus Professor of Ecumenics at the Lutheran School of Theology at Chicago.

From 1946 to 1953 Professor Tobias was Assistant Director of the Department of Inter-Church Aid and Service to Refugees of the World Council of Churches with special responsibilities for East Europe and the Orthodox churches. In that capacity he has visited frequently among the Orthodox churches all over Europe and the Near East, linking churches in the West with Orthodox churches in consultations, exchange programs, and in ministries of relief and reconstruction during and after wars, earthquakes, and other disasters. One of his tasks was to observe the ways Communist governments were taking over in East Europe after World War II, eventually publishing his findings in his *Communist-Christian Encounter in East Europe.*

For his work in Greece, Professor Tobias was decorated by King Paul of Greece as Commander of the Royal Order of Phoenix, and in Yugoslavia he was decorated by Patriarchs German and Pavel with the Order of St. Sava, the highest honor bestowed by the Serbian Orthodox Church. In Geneva he was awarded the "Key to the City."

Since his return to the United States, Professor Tobias has continued his contacts and visits with the Orthodox in East Europe and has served on numerous committees, commissions, and boards of the World Council of Churches, the National Council of the Churches of Christ in the USA, the Lutheran Church in America, and other ecumenical and international organizations and programs. Beginning in 1983 he cochaired the sessions of the second round of Lutheran-Orthodox Dialogue in North America and has coedited the two-volume report of that Dialogue together with the late Father John Meyendorff, Dean of St. Vladimir's Orthodox Theological Seminary in Crestwood, New York. Now retired, Professor Tobias lives with his wife Trudy in Racine, Wisconsin.

Heaven on Earth: A Lutheran-Orthodox Odyssey
by Robert Tobias

Questions for Study Groups

Forewords and Introduction
What prompted the 16th-century Lutheran reformers to seek contact with the Orthodox? Why did the Orthodox want contact with the Lutherans? How might it have made a difference in Lutheran-Orthodox relations if there had been earlier contact, before Lutherans had to defend their Augsburg Confession and before pluralism among the heirs of the Reformation further complicated its witness? How open is communication now? How can we facilitate that? What are the options for us now, in North America?

Chapter 1. Boulevards and Village Squares
Spiritually speaking, are we "already where we're going"? If we feel deeply that we aren't, why? If we feel that we are, does that mean that we are fully arrived, or are there still limitations in our pilgrimage? St. Paul writes (I Cor. 7:29–31) that we should live *as though (hos)* we are already where we're going *because (gar)* we are already where we're going. Yet he writes (Phil. 3:14), "I press on ..." Already? Or not yet? What is it that must be completed, for what reason, and in what company? What differences can we see in even the very basic approaches, respectively, of "East" and "West"?

Chapter 2. Churchyards and Battlefields
Are there times when we sense that the "dead" are not, after all, absent from us and the world we live in? Describe such experiences. What do we understand the phrase in the eucharistic liturgy to mean: "... with angels and archangels and with all the company of heaven we laud and magnify Thy glorious name ..."? Does that include our close departed ones? Would that mean that the Church Triumphant and the Church Militant are not wholly separated? If not separated, how would we know and show that? With shared prayers? With prayer candles? With icons? Does the rest of creation participate in any way with us in worship? Why? How would we describe "liturgy" in this under-standing? What does St. Paul mean (Rom. 8:19) by "The whole creation waits with an ardent desire the coming of the sons of God"?

Chapter 3. Icons and Ornaments
Is there anything about the natural creation that gives it some sacred quality? If so, what? As Scripture says of our bodies, is the whole

1

creation in any sense God's temple? Is it an affront to God if we reject creation as evil or unworthy of salvation? In our own behavior, how can we distinguish between respecting creation's sanctity and the idolatry of things? Does "classical Lutheranism" have more in common with the Eastern Orthodox, or with iconoclasts and "Puritan" strains in Christianity?

Chapter 4. The Liturgy and the Clock
Is it the gathering at a special time and place that makes the church Church, or is it always gathered, anywhere, everywhere as a "cosmic family reunion"? Is the "sacrifice of God" just what happened on Good Friday on Golgotha—or is it an eternal happening, not limited to a specific event in a specific location and time? If it's a "forever happening," why then do we have in the Eucharist a specific time and piece of bread and wine? If God's Presence and action are always and everywhere, why not take communion as a sip of wine at a local bar, or why not see golfing or mountain climbing as worship? What is the "specialness" of worship in *special time (kairos)* and places? Why? Where? And how? And how is that specialness related to "Real Presence" and all other experiences everywhere?

Chapter 5. Scripture? Or Tradition?
There are many ways of reading Scripture. One may read it for spiritual enrichment, or as an answer book for life's problems, or as illumination of historical events and human biography, or as an authoritative guide for religious matters, or as a centerpiece around which the extended biblical community gathers for ongoing conversation. Which of these accents, or others, takes precedence? With what differing results? There are also different kinds of tradition: e.g., established customs, or *Living* Tradition still underway. How do they differ? How are different kinds of "scripture" and different kinds of tradition interrelated? How is the Holy Spirit involved in that? The church and its councils?

Chapter 6. Love Me? Feed My Sheep
Given the evidence in this chapter and in Chapter 3 (Icons and Ornaments), does the phrase "the Church of Captivity" as applied to the Orthodox churches take on special meaning? How might this temper Western Christianity's revived drive for "evangelism" in the East? As Lutherans and Orthodox we do not, intentionally, proselytize one another. Are there ways we, as congregations, families, synods, and seminaries in America, could encourage and support one another locally and nationally, as we have done so effectively abroad? Can you suggest some specifics?

2

Chapter 7. Winter and Spring

What are our personal experiences with or in the midst of tragedy and death? What special signs of new life have we seen in the midst of death? If drawing a "flow" chart, how would we connect Jesus' life, death, resurrection, ascension, return, presence, and our own? Are there significant differences here between Orthodox and Lutheran understandings? If so, are the differences to be avoided, or shared for mutual learning and support?

Chapter 8. American Culture and Our Commonalities

If, as has been said, American Lutherans are becoming more hierarchical and American Orthodox are becoming more congregational, is the base of those changes American cultural custom--or a clearer understanding of the God-given nature of the church on the part of both? What are the benefits of each trend, and of their complementarities? Do we regard the state and church as both being under God but mutually supportive and corrective of each other? Do we decide what is right by whether it works and is acceptable in the marketplace, or by whether it springs from God's will and grace? Do we understand God's presence among us as being for the purpose of doing something *to* us, or *for* us, or because it is God's earnest desire to dwell among us? Are our clergy regarded as employees and CEOs of the congregation, or instruments of God, relating each of us to all everywhere and all to the triune God? Do we look forward expectantly, pray and work that we shall one day be joined fully and visibly in the fullness of the whole church universal? How do we do that, and with what accents of legitimate differentiation, to the blessing of all?

Chapter 9. The Real of Earth and Heaven

How do we understand the relation between spirit and matter today? Are spirit and matter diametrically opposed, one good, the other evil, or is ours a unified creation with all-inclusive interdependencies and complementarities as well as differentiations? Is there any sacredness about matter? Can/does matter serve as bearer of spirit? Of spirituality? If so, how? What about cancer, or man-eating sharks? Is God *really* present in, with, and under our *real* world? All the time, or only for special moments, such as Holy Communion? Is there a *real* difference, beyond our perception?

Chapter 10. Roundtables and Courtrooms

With reference to blackbird and hummingbird styles, which is the "style" of my life? Is it pushy, combative, cerebral, perhaps cold and heartless? Warm, gentle, caring, with heart? Or a mix? What does this have to say about the "life style" manifested in our respective faith traditions—and how things are done in America? What about our family, our congregation, our community; do we have a distinct style? Is it, or the mix, a style we like? That others can accept, or like and encourage? Is there a "God style"?

Chapter 11. Mystery and Theology

What do I mean by "knowledge" and "knowing"? How large a place is there for mystery in my thinking and living? Do I expect it to grow or to disappear with time, discovery, and learning? Do I expect to resolve the problems, puzzles, unknowns, and mysteries of life? Which? And which not? Is my understanding of God and "things divine" a knowable quantity? If Truth is more than logical noncontradiction, if it is relationship, undividedness, and companionship, does that rule out mystery? Or perhaps enlarge it? Can we reconcile the East's "mystery approach" with the West's more typically "rational systems," with so-called "scientific" methodology? What do I expect of theology and theologians?

Chapter 12. Heaven on Earth

What is our expectation of "heaven"? Is it a place or a condition mostly awaited after life? Or is there some way in which heaven is already here, and we live and rejoice in it? Already? Not yet? Both? If in any measure "already," how do we describe it? Participate in it? And with whom? In comparison to our Lutheran-Orthodox Dialogue, is our primary concern about salvation with the "what" or the "how" of salvation? How do we define or describe each, the "what" and the "how"? Or might our concern be to know the "who" and the "why" of salvation? Assuming that it is God who gives salvation, how would we understand God's "why"? Has that any bearing on "what" and "how"? Would that put a different "spin" on our prayer life? Our worship? What can we do now to make way for the fullness of God's grace and his church? Could we detail a list, put task forces to work on some shared guidelines, and help activate shared programs locally, regionally, or nationally, in consultation with our respective synod or nationwide ecumenical committees, or with our North American Dialogue commission?

(May be reproduced for study groups.)